The Village Pariah

Imali J. Abala

First Edition: June 2024
Published by: Nsemia Inc. Publishers (www. nsemia.com)

Edited: Andrew Nyongesa
Cover Concept: Author
Cover Illustration: Abel Murumba
Cover Design: Linda Kiboma
Layout Design: Bethsheba Nyabuto

Note for Librarians:
A cataloguing record for this book is available from Kenya National Library Services

ISBN: 978-9914-760-11-8

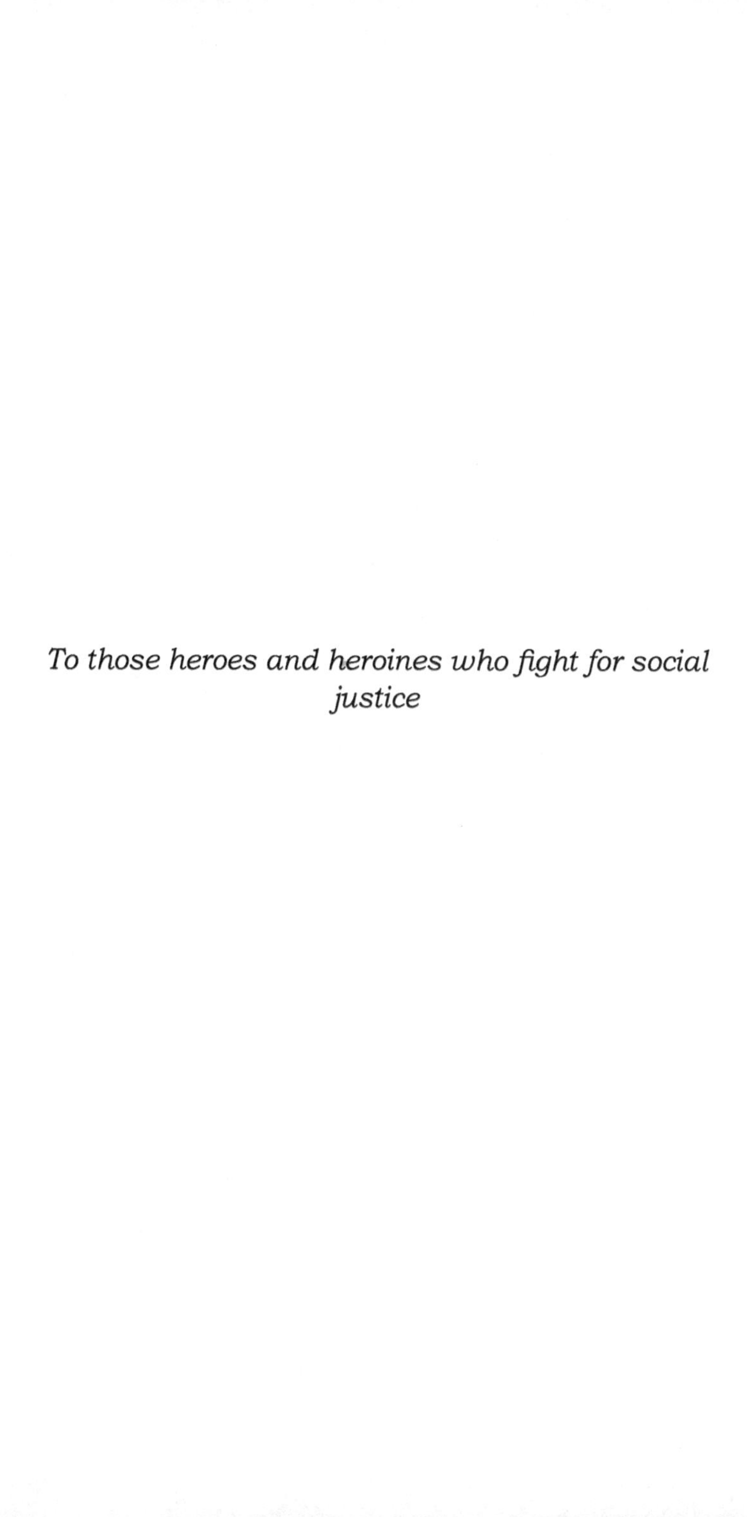

To those heroes and heroines who fight for social justice

Table of Contents

Prologue

Rosie was rattled from her afternoon siesta with a loud bang,

But with her senses dulled with sleep, she didn't see the looming danger,

Of a man, ill-tempered, running towards her like a charging bull

Ready to destroy a life; much like she had his destroyed.

He brandished a sharpened machete that glittered in the sun.

His eyes were red hot, as red as cayenne pepper, and his mouth . . .

Yes, his mouth frothed at the corners. Not even the Almighty

Could his resolve change, unaware revenge is a fool's paradise!

In that twinkling, he knew he held her worthless life in his hands,

Not even the screams of her voice, alerting others of her danger

Could her destiny alter! She who had caused others sadness,

Deserved every punishment that came her way; call it cold justice!

And the man's justice, he an avenging angel, came to her swiftly,

As he ran as fast as lightning with little time left for any felt fear.

So, her feeble heart yielded to this merciless
mercenary of peace.

And then, the light in her eyes went out as he, with
precision,

Exacted his revenge to the earth's darkening against
a sunless sky,

But whence she had rested, the hungry earth
soaked a pool of red,

And when the man emerged from his troublesome
daydream,

His body was soaked wet as beads of sweat streaked
over his brow!

1

Whispers from the Land Beyond

Mama always told me telling on others
Does not build character.
I disagreed because, sometimes,
It is just to tell on others,
Open that vault of their past secrets,
Though, in so doing, tell it honestly.
Nothing more, but the truth!
Not the twisted kind meant to hurt.
A hoax? Fake and ill-intentioned.
Mine, Mama, to be precise, is pure truth.
I trust in its candour, of its double-edged nature:
To liberate the innocent,
And unmask the evil doers, the very reason
I am telling on Rosie Kasuvo,
The Beautiful One, beloved by a few,
And despised by many!

Mama always said,
If you can't say anything to one's face,
Keep your mouth shut,
Sealed like a vault; for if not,
You won't know what ghosts you'll unleash,
Or let fly out in the process.

I listened silently and looked on.
Maybe she was right!

Stop your foolishness and gossip,
You hear? She would say.
It is unbecoming of you!
She warned in her stern motherly voice.

Her words to my ears rang louder and clearer.
I didn't listen then.
I must confess!
But I can still hear the sweet melody
      of her reproving voice.
Mama has been ten years long gone.
Though her life may have faded away,
Much like a passing shadow,
Her words will, in me, forever live!

I don't mean Mama any disrespect,
Not heeding her advice that is,
But come along with me,
Accompany me on this journey,
Of a past in remembrance!
Let me tell you about Rosie,
The Beautiful One,
As she came to be known.
Though, as Nyasaye is my witness,
She was no more a mistress of deception
Than a woman whose heart seemed beautiful,

As beautiful as a seraph's dream.
Trust me, I know this to be true!
I don't mean her any harm, none.
Her fate need not rest solely in my words.
Her actions are the yardstick of her measure,
And nothing more,
Not even Eliab's words, my nephew,
The sole soul and architect of this tale.
For he was its truest custodian!

When Rosie, the Beautiful one,
Made her appearance in Ngoroke
     on May 15, 1963,
A beautiful Wednesday morning,
The trumpets of the nation's freedom
     from British rule
Were at fever pitch!
While for Adonis Lidede,
Her prospective loving husband,
Bellowed bells of their knotted marital bliss.
His heart, dulled by love, beat in frenzy
Like thrums of an *isugudi* drummer
     who had lost his skill,
Beating his drum in disharmony
     on a *waragi* filled belly
Whose mind, liquor dulled,
No longer knew reason.
His tongue, as heavy as lead,
Slurred his words—

I am a . . ma a r r i eed ma . . man—
As his hands flapped about
Like a broken-winged bird.

That day, when Adonis married Rosie,
It wasn't festive—no dancing,
No singing, no ululating,
But the sun rose, showering the village anew
With her elegance,
Having dusted away the blackness of night.

We rejoiced!
Uncle had won a beautiful trophy,
Unware he had dug his own grave,
Much like a neighbor who had, unwittingly,
Bought a casket for a daughter's burial,
Having received word of her demise,
Only to be its guest hours later.
His end, an outcome of a daughter's living.

When Adonis' sun fell westward,
Showering the horizon with its golden glow,
Its amber hue fused with red,
As red as petals of a red rose in a plush brush,
Adonis' rose, sharp and thorny,
Was Rosie's sharp barbed words,
Which, in due time, mercilessly tore at his heart,
Shredded it to pieces and discarded him
Much like useless bagasse at a funeral pyre!

Those who chanced to meet her,
Claimed Rosie was a woman of faith,
A churchgoer, but the Beautiful One,
Whose sweet-scented words
Made hearts thrum in lust,
Lived a faithless life,
For she was no saint to speak of,
But a devil in human clothing.
Those with lustful hearts,
Unknowingly, found her irresistible.
Her grand entrance anywhere
Was never a dull moment.
Countless eyes drawn to her beauty,
Gaped wide, unshifting in her presence.
Yet, these very longing eyes,
knew not her infinite unworthiness,
And wallowed in the mystery of her being.
For the Beautiful One was unworthy of conquest,
But only a few knew it!
Her large round brown piercing eyes,
As round as Sodom apples,
Smiled my sorrow and joy.
I wasn't alone. Others under her spell fell,
A truth, which she exploited.
Whoever turned away such a beauty?

Many have frowned against my desire,
To tell on Rosie, the Beautiful One,
Me, Adonis' niece, and Eliab's cousin,
But their disagreeableness was unfounded.

Rosie was not a sweet, scented rose,
As sweet as the eye-catching rose bush,
Vibrant, and scented to the nose.
She never was then nor is she now.
She is evil. As evil as the biblical Herod
A man who initiated the murder
Of infants in Bethlehem!
A fallen angel of Ngoroke Village,
Whose evil deeds were greater than Lucifer's,
The fabled son of Aurora and Cephalus,
God's prideful angel, fallen from grace!
That is who Rosie, the Beautiful One, is!
Ngoroke's fallen angel that never was,
    a village pariah,
Whose misdeeds are the reason
For my telling on her . . .

Rosie, the Beautiful One,
Sweet-tongued, can't be missed in Ngoroke!
Whenever she walks into a room,
With confidence and sassiness,
Her curvy voluptuous figure,
Is a sight to behold!
The young and old, women and men,
All fall under her spell,
As the pupils of her eyes,
Large brown sparkle under the sun
    Like diamonds.
Their earthy hue, window to her soul,
Mask her heart's darkness.

I have often wondered why
These magnificently divine eyes
Could harbour so much evil!
How could these very sweet,
And kind eyes, maim, or take lives
As they dart lovingly, back-and-forth,
Glistening under the sun's glow?
I am as petrified as to how
They mask her essence
She, the embodiment of evil.

Forgive me, Mama!
Beauty is only, but skin deep,
As deep as Rosie's beauty!
Outside, sparkling, and radiant
While inside,
She is as rotten as a rotting fruit.
Rotten like a worm-infested mango
That has fallen off Grandma's mango tree.
Too good to eat but repulsing to the bite.
A truth unbeknownst to Adonis,
Who bit bait to his own damnation,
And now gags at the pungent smelly Rosie,
Too repulsive to the nose to radiate love.
For the smell of her ill-tempered ways,
Too, are obvious to any observer,
Like the smell of a rotting carcass
Often a feast for a vulture's delight!

Adonis, her mate, wasn't blind
When he chose her for a wife.
He, like all of us,
Did her rottenness see,
Unmasked the blinders off his cloudy eyes
Saw her sharp thorns that stabbed at anything,
And everything in her path.
She never discriminated,
Family and friends,
All fell under her spell and prey!

How could a silent female slayer
Cloaked like a beautiful soul be shielded?
Not even Mama could vouch for this,
That Rosie, the magnificent,
Couldn't alter her fate!
For she had set in motion unfathomable
And irreversible chain of events—
She, the devil in human clothing—
Of which Baba in his sermons didn't preach.
Yes, Baba, a pious praying man, often,
Sermonized about angels and devils on Sunday.
So, in my mind's eye,
I pictured angels as white-winged saints,
That floated above us, our guardians,
But imagined devils as fearful giants
Cloaked in red with red devilish eyes
Beset to tame our souls to our damnation.
I, in my naiveté, did, without question
Believed Baba's words to be so, never knowing

Devils weren't intangible beings beyond our grasp.

Yet, now, I make a solemn proclamation:

Devils do, indeed, among us live,

Clothed in suits, not amorphous outliers!

Truly, the banality of evil was too close us,

More so than Baba ever preached!

Our Rosie, the charming Rosie,

Whose smile was as delightful

    as April rose, was its avatar.

Her copper ever-glistening pupils

    held her evil secrets,

Secrets enough to make hearts recoil,

And hairs on bodies stand like porcupine spikes,

Ready to shield and kill in a moment's notice.

Mama, pardon me for telling on Rosie.

What a *just* song to sing

For the fallen and rotting rose!

2

Love Is Never Really Blind

Mama would be disappointed in me
For telling on Rosie, the village pariah,
Whose desire to be loved led her to Ngoroke,
A village fortified to the east with giant boulders,
The sleeping hills, Nyasaye's gift to Logooli people—
The everlasting creator of all living things—
And a reminder of His ever-present might.
Yet,
Upon her arrival,
She didn't know the truth Mama warned us about.
That the village had many eyes and many ears.
They see and hear everything,
The good, the bad, the ugly!
This was the reason it was a vibrant community,
But, at the same time,
Was fraught with rumourmongers,
Who disregarded others' needs
For assumed harmonious living,
And their mantra:
We are one and in one, we live!

Before she became Ngoroke's village pariah,
Rosie, the Beautiful One,
Was her family's pride.

A woman who came into being in an era
    of great changes,
When parents, bug-bitten by the education bug
Sent their children to school to taste the fruits of
    uhuru.
That for the benefit of family and their viability
It was their obvious reality,
But never lost sight of one truth:
That a girl's first duty was her natural rights,
    wife and mother.
That her value rested in her dowry,
Token of her net worth!

Yet,
In her heart,
Rosie knew her duty was her yoke,
Not her liberty!
Her schooling was only a minor distraction
    of her formative years,
But when she came of age,
And the doors of marital bliss opened,
Her parents, against her wish,
Did collude to halt her studies,
Having a suitor of good repute
    pegged for her future joy,
A decision to which she had no privy—
As was the norm in such matters—
For her parents who never thought she,
Like all mortals, had a mind,

Faltered in their resolve to marry her off
        to a man of their choosing.
But she, despite her family's choice,
Would her heart follow,
Having met Adonis Lidede,
A man of her dreams,
To whom her heart
She had freely yielded.

Their unexpected affair was a tale
Of romantic love born in youth,
Which Adonis, with candour and bravado,
        had made known to all.
Those whose trumpet ears
Gobbled-up words of their holy meeting,
Of the moment when his eyes,
On the beauty, had landed by chance,
As he loitered in her village amid friends.
Thunderstruck at her sighting,
A moment forever frozen in his mind,
Which in response,
He, like most men his age,
Did the natural thing they did,
He whistled mischievously!
And she,
Drawn to the melody of his whistling,
Stopped in her tracks,
Turned in his direction,
And craned her neck to see the boisterous whistler.

She, too, like him,

Became smitten by the young lad's sparkling
    beauty.

Who could contest this illusionary notion,

Of "Love at first sight?"

Therefore,

Inevitable it became

That Adonis would defy traditions.

That when his eyes had fallen upon her,

A luscious plum beauty,

Rosie, the Beautiful One,

Whose radiant eyes sparkled under the sun,

He knew as Nyasaye was his witness,

She was the one and no other!

Her radiant ebony skin,

As smooth as silk, glittery, and divine,

Made his heart race,

Like a marathon runner's pounding at a meet.

In that fleeting moment,

He knew no other option

But possess the jewel that,

For seasons he had longed,

A choice to which no one had privy.

Not even his meddlesome parents,

Villagers or relatives could interfere!

For they were as blind

And as deaf to the lovers' love affair,

And let it flounder in the darkness,

Of their thoughts and hearts.

So,
It came to pass that their pact
Needed no parental blessings,
Which they deemed unnecessary
For the Almighty had destined it.
Besides, with the winds of change
Across the nation fanning individuality,
Nothing, save death,
could foil this sweet love.
No investigations of the bride
Or groom was necessary,
A slap in the face against the timeless
        investigative customary norm:
To ascertain and vouch for a bride,
Or groom's character or family,
To eliminate any doubt as to whether
Any abnormalities or deviancy existed:
        of epilepsy
        of madness
        of murder
        or witchcraft.
This oversight made me wonder
If a union borne out this violation
Could survive the test of time!

She, like him, was charmed.
That he did her acquaintance make
And, lured by his mesmerizing beauty,
        chocolate brown,
Tall and with muscles flexed,

Did her heart win with a smile?
His teeth, ivory white,
Did her heart tame and steal forever,
Her undying love for him
She vowed as her forever, nothing less.
What a divine commitment to a union
      sealed with an erotic kiss!
With a tip of his hat,
He did his proposal make.
And she, without hesitation,
Gave her unreserved consent.
So, without notice and much ado,
She did make her exit from home!
All this was to her father's chagrin,
And horror-stricken realization.
That his daughter had gone
Left home for some unknown destination!
A mystery resolved at the break of dawn
      of the next day.
When Adonis had, as a norm,
Sent an emissary to her folks,
Quelling the mystery of her unexplained
      absence from home,
For no one could, even if they tried,
Contest matters of the heart.
Not even a father's iron-fisted clutch
      against a daughter's heart.
And so, it came to pass
That no one could alter their fate!

At least, that was what the villagers
    thought and believed.

Yet,
Not all loves are meant for silver bells,
But the bitter brazen alarm tolls as would,
    in due time,
Mark an end to Adonis and Rosie,
    the Beautiful One's union
Eliab, his nephew,
Bitter of heart, held a key in its telling!

3

Broken Ties

Adonis, Rosie's handsome husband,
Turned out to be a scumbag!
Never living true to his natural duties,
Which husbands must fulfill for viability,
Yet even scumbags don't deserve his type of end,
Not one bit. Not the karma that followed
     in his retirement!

Like most men in the village,
His long-awaited accolades of married life
     stroked his ego,
Like the thrums of a guitar player
     to his instrument.
Short-lived, it was an inch's worth.
The impact of his stroking, on spectators,
Not noteworthy for he, without her regard,
Left home weeks into their union,
Lured by the glamour of city life,
A sweet apple too enticing to ignore the bite.
Eliazar, *the* educated man of Ngoroke,
Was to blame for this allure.
For he had, in a whiff,
Promised many men the moon,
But delivered dust instead,

Dangling the steak of freedom
Soliciting many a man's departure.
Beguiled by the promised bounty,
Had hope a fool's perfect paradise offered.
That they, too, could cash in
When the fruits of independence came,
But these fruits were more meagre
Than wanton richness promised—
Slaving on European farms
Be their norm unworthy of the sacrifice.

The raggedness of Ngoroke village
A life fraught with poverty,
Was and will always be
A bitter pill for the educated,
Whose tongues, tongue-tied,
Because of their scanty living,
Clogged their sane thinking:
That the joy of village life wasn't for them.
Yet, this very raggedness,
Emblem of their being,
Was the bedrock of their communal existence,
Where one's action was never a private affair,
But held to public scrutiny,
With nowhere to hide
Or shelter the self against all watchful eyes.

As Rosie and Adonis' hearts
Thrummed their undying love,
Under the watchful gaze of family and village,

Adonis, like most men his age,
Without notice left home for city life,
And sentenced her unduly
To the communal prison of Ngoroke.
Not foray in nature, though duly,
It might as well have been!
Their ecstasy, her woe,
Defied the joys of their nuptial bliss,
Their coveted measure for success,
Was greater than the folly of his actions,
Of leaving her,
For their benefit and family.
It was meant to be their glory,
While Loise, his mother,
Was glad that her son
Had brought home a helper,
And hoped, in due time,
She would her natural duties fulfill:
Fill her homestead with his offspring,
A family's hope, pride,
And joy as was expected.
She was wrong, at first anyway!

When Adonis left Rosie,
A life of loneliness became her norm.
Thus, she immersed herself in village life
    and its communal living,
Performing her duties to Loise,
Her mother-in-law, as expected and norm.
Day in and day out,

She tilled the land and cooked her in-laws' meals,
Not having been married long enough to earn
    the right to her own kitchen.
All the while, she was hopeful Adonis
Would return home to reclaim her.
She was wrong! For her benefit,
She abandoned herself to the church,
Becoming one among ardent worshipers
Who prostrated at salvation's altar,
Daily and there sought faith,
Which Mama often said was like sunrise at dawn,
That gleamed brighter than anything Rosie knew.
It birthed her daily hope!
And hope was all Rosie had,
Even as she became a choir leader.
Oftentimes, her voice rang louder than
    the echoes of her beguiled mind
And to Nyasaye in her singing and prayers
Did she her heart's desires pour,
Soliciting His intervention
For Adonis' return home
In one piece: not in pieces!
A saintly woman she became,
Finding nobility among like-minded folks.

Forthwith,
Religion permeated every fibre
Of her being and elevated her status.
A lay leader she became,
And served many souls needing Nyasaye's Grace,

Yet, her prayers for Adonis' heart,
To find its path home, fell short.
And so, her prayers, like her faith,
Showed no evidence of fruition.
And soon, this very faith,
Which had anchored her in adulthood
Became as dead as her faith
In her marriage and humanity.

By and by,
The delight of her youthfulness
      and unrequited love,
Which was her ill fate,
Birthed her mischievousness.
Though, perhaps,
It was with her all along.
As envy, the folly of humankind
And vice, moved hearts against her.
Nonetheless, unfulfilled in flesh,
Her assumed 'barren' womb
Gave way to her first foibles,
An accusation I must have missed.
But Mama, who never spoke ill of others,
Told me all I needed to know,
About Rosie, the Beautiful One!

Why did Rosie become the village pariah?
      [I once asked Mama one evening,
        When she and I were preparing supper.]
Because she can't keep her skirt down, she said.

Why is that? I said.

How the hell should I know? she said.

> *[She fell silent for a moment. I followed suit.*
> *I knew Mama didn't mean to be brash with*
> *   me.*
> *Mama was never brash with people, not even*
> *   me.*
> *She was a gentle soul, as gentle as a sheep,*
> *But how could she broach such a delicate*
> *   subject?]*

With her skirt up, Mama said,

She ruled men as Nyasaye rules the earth.

> *[I tried to understand what she meant,*
> *But her point evaded me for years.]*

Your uncle has deserted her, she added.

Is that the only reason why

She can't keep her skirt down? I said.

I don't know, she said.

Good wives keep their skirts down. Not up.

Oh! I said.

Remember this, Mama said.

Maybe there were other reasons!

Like what? I said puzzled,

Trying to understand the skirt business.

People say Adonis doesn't support her, she said.

It is like she doesn't exist to him.

Why is that? I said.

Aah! she said with a hint of irritation.

Uvuchima vujila nguza vukusambiila ki?

Oh, I see! I said.

But honestly, I didn't get it.

Mama liked to speak in riddles.

You'll understand when you grow up.

I shrugged my shoulders!

> *[She didn't say anything. Neither did I.*
>
> *Time, between us, stood still, deathly still.*
>
> *I tried to translate her riddle in my simple mind.*
>
> *Why should "Ugali without vegetables burn me?"*
>
> *My attempted translation of her riddle was far*
> *from the truth.*
>
> *I knew that wasn't what she meant, so I let it be!*
>
> *Perhaps Mama was right!*
>
> *I will understand it when I grow up.*
>
> *Yet, even now in my adult life,*
>
> *I only take it to mean:*
>
> *Mind your own business!*
>
> *That was it and nothing more.]*

Tell you what, Mama said.

What Mama, I said.

Your uncle will come back in time!

If you say so, I said.

Mark my words! She said and meant it.

He'll be back.

> *[Yes. Mama was right.*
>
> *Uncle did return home after years.*
>
> *He was a broken man,*
>
> *Not the carefree person I knew,*
>
> *But the chasm between him*
>
> *And Rosie was beyond repair.]*

That evening,

When we finished cooking,
We ate our supper in silence,
Yet, inwardly, I wondered
What in the Devil's name
Had possessed Adonis
To become Ngoroke's mysterious ghost!

4

When the Dead Talk, The Living Cringe

I believe there is goodness

In people and the world.

That, even evil folks,

In their darkest hour, have scruples,

But not Rosie, she was of a different breed.

Mama told me something else,

A shocking and unspoken truth

About her lasting the test of time.

Mama and I were seated under

The shade of the jacaranda tree.

It was a fine afternoon and time

Didn't seem to be at a standstill.

Hours melted away like the sun's

Hazy light into the horizon's blue.

Do you know another thing Rosie did?

  Mama said.

  [We had not spoken about Rosie in a while.

  I wasn't probing her for anything about her at
    all.

  Perhaps,

  It was the idleness of our late afternoon day.

  When she mentioned her name,

I didn't know why, but my ears were wide open
to take in all she had to say.]
It is one of her darkest secrets, Mama warned.
What did she do this time? I said in dismay.
They claim Rosie killed your niece!
What! Who said that? I asked.

[I didn't ask her who 'they' were.
She didn't have to tell me.
I knew them already!
The village had deep tentacles.
It saw and heard everything.
For it had already stirred
the slanderous pot against Rosie,
Started the unspoken whispers
Of her misdeeds, true or false.
Now, she had to bear
the scars of their hurtful words.]

How did she do it Mama? I said.
Perhaps, I should not fill your mind,
With this foolishness! she said.
Silence followed her thought.
I looked on, weighing her words carefully.
Maybe I shouldn't tell you this, she said.
What good will it do?

[I scratched my head in puzzlement.
Hadn't she already set a trap for me?
Hadn't I, with open arms, eyes,
Ears and fallen into it?
I let these thoughts race through my mind,
but refrained from voicing them.]

Knowledge is power Mama! I said.

True, Mama said.

In ignorance, I might vanquish Mama, I said.

Well, if you insist, I'll tell you!

Mama said in a stern voice.

Please, Mama, I said, eager with anticipation.

Rosie, whose womb was as barren as a rock,

As folks thought, envied your brother.

Why did she envy my brother? I said.

Because Nyasaye blessed him with daughters,
    Mama said.

Oh! I said.

She doesn't have a girl child, Mama said.
    [This was an odd thing to grasp.
    Logooli people value boys over girls.
    That is how it used to be in the old days,
    Though, I believe it is still so today.]

What does her envy have to do

With my niece's death? I said.

Malice knows no boundaries, my child,
    Mama said.

Oh! I said. I didn't have to imagine her malice.

If you must know, she said, I will tell you.

Please do! I said,

Hoping she would unravel Rosie's mystery.

On one condition, she said.

What may that be? I said.

You must promise me
    never to tell a soul about it.

I won't tell a soul, I said.

For I was earnest in my promise!
>*[Mama fell silent,*
>*and looked at me—eye-to-eye.*
>*Her eyes pierced mine*
>*And cut through me like a knife!*
>*Mama seemed to be*
>*weighing her next words carefully.*
>*Still, I wondered if she doubted*
>*The sincerity of my promise.]*

What happened?
I said with my curiosity piqued.
>*[Mama cleared her throat,*
>*but remained silent.*
>*I looked on afraid*
>*To disturb her train of thought.]*

Remember, she said.
Your niece was in class seven when she died!
Yeap! I know it, I said.
How can I forget the first death in our family?
She was a very brilliant girl,
Mama said ignoring my last sentence.
Sure! What *really* happened to her? I said.
>*[I was away when this happened.]*

It all started when she stopped at Rosie's house
>on her way from school.

How did you know she did that? I said.
She told her mother when she returned home,
>Mama said.

How is it then that Rosie killed her?
She served her fermented porridge,

Which your niece loved very much.
What? I gasped. Porridge? Of all things?
> *[I must confess! I hate porridge.*
> *I would rather die than drink porridge.*
> *I had a lion's share of it*
> *While in secondary school,*
> *for which I only have horror stories.]*
Of course, she did!
She drank Rosie's porridge to satisfaction.
Wow, I said. Porridge of all meals!
When she returned home, Mama said,
She was a baked goose,
Destined for the grave!
> *[Like any simpleton that I was,*
> *I pictured my niece in an oven baking.]*
Why was that? I said.
She had one complaint, Mama said.
What was it? I said.
Her tummy ached.
Wow! I said.
Rosie must have added
Something in her porridge, Mama said...
Could it have been something else
That led to her tummy ache? I said.
No! Absolutely not, she said affirmatively.
How did she kill her then? I said.
Poison dear, she said.
They said *she* poisoned her
    with her porridge.
Who said it? I said

The village *knows* everything my child, she added.
They *know!* Remember this, *they* Know!
How did they know? I said.
They know, hear, and see *things*, Mama said.
Really? I said in disbelief.
Though I *knew* she was right!
Yes, she said.
They know things you can't even imagine.
What kind of poison did she use Mama?
I don't know, she said.
Some said it was *imbiring'ong'o—*
Some unknown poison.

> *[The light in Mama's eyes dimmed slightly*
> *While I thought, she was maybe fibbing.*
> *She fell silent, allowing a moment*
> > *of deep contemplation to elapse.*
> *My razor-sharp eyes remained fixated on her.*
> *Motionless, she dropped her gaze to the ground.*
> *I sat stock-still waiting for her*
> > *to unveil secrets of her tale.*
> *I hoped she would tell me the meaning*
> > *of imbiring'ong'o.*
> *She didn't and to this day,*
> > *its meaning still evades me.*
> *When her lips fell open in speech,*
> > *she didn't disappoint.*
> *Her chest heaved,*
> > *And her voice trembled in her telling and.]*

With one glance at her,

Her parents knew the girl was in trouble.
How did she look? I said.
She walked slouched forward
      with her hands wrapped around her belly.
I see, I said.
    [I tried to picture the girl's image
    in her forward stoop writhing in pain.
    Poor girl. Poor little girl!]
What happened next, I said.
Your brother rushed her to hospital, Mama said.
Did he go alone, I said.
No. Your cousin Aluda went with him!
Wololo! I said.
With cheetah speed, she said.
The pair ran down the hill to Maseno Hospital.
The spring in their feet, though measured,
Wasn't fast enough to save her, Mama said.
    [I didn't hear anything else Mama said for a
      minute,
    My mind consumed with the image of the pair,
    As they dashed down the narrow footpath to
      the hospital.
    I pictured their descent down the hill's
      treacherous terrain,
    With its demanded caution,
    A slip carried with it a danger threat!]
It was too late, she said,
With a quiver in her tone.
How did they know it was poison
      that killed her? I said.

It was the frothing at the corners
     of her mouth, she said.
The girl cried of tummy ache nonstop . . .
And that, if you ask me,
Was a sign she had consumed something bad!
Oh dear! I said.
Doctors tested her stomach contents
During her autopsy.
Oh! I see. Is that how they knew,
     for *sure*, she was poisoned?
Yes! Her organs—lungs, liver,
And kidneys—were all destroyed.
Oh, dear! Poor thing, I said.
They said she died of arsenic poisoning,
     Mama said,
But who knows the truth about these things,
But Nyasaye Himself.
     [Mama let out another big sigh.
     She didn't add another word for a while.
     I was muted by this revelation.
     I felt a cool draft of wind nip my skin.]
I hope she didn't suffer much, I said.
She went very fast, Mama said.
Did the Sub-chief or Chief investigate the matter?
Yes, Mama said.
She dropped her eyes to the ground.
     [A pregnant moment of silence fell between us.
     I closed my eyes, but my ears remained wide
       open,

> *As wide as those of our Ngorokean village*
>   *dwellers,*
>
> *For they never miss a sound, not even a*
>   *stinky fart!]*

Some people are too crafty, she said.
Craftier than a fox. Can you believe that?
Rosie outfoxed the Chief, she said.
Her voice cracked at this admission.
Did they inspect her house for the poison?
Everywhere, turned her house inside out?
I asked.
My child, she said. They found *nothing*.
Absolutely nothing. Absolutely nothing.
Oh, Nyasaye! How unbelievable! I exclaimed.
Not even a sliver of something? I said.
Nope. *Nada!* she said.
Not one drop? I said.
Her house was as clean as a whistle, she said.
She fell silent once more.
A cool drifting wind passed.
With your niece dead, she said,
We had no witness to her crime.
What about postmortem? I protested.
Didn't it mean anything?
Yes, but nobody saw her poison your niece!
Then, nothing came out of this inquiry.
No, but in my heart, I *knew* she did it.
The dead had already spoken.

> *[If you are wondering why Mama is telling me*
>   *these things,*

> *I was not home when my niece died, but in*
> *school.*
> *It was my final year and sitting for my fourth*
> *form exams.*
> *Family thought it best I remained uninformed.*
> *My presence couldn't have brought the dead*
> *back to life.*]

Do you know another strange thing
    that happened? Mama asked.
No. What happened?
I opened my eyes and looked at her.
After we brought your niece's corpse home,
    the dead spoke! She said.
Yes, Mama, but how can the dead speak,
That is if they are dead?
    Call me a doubting Thomas.
The Beautiful One came to view her body!
She said.
Isn't that a custom? I said.
Yes, but as she leaned in to view the body,
    the corpse cried! Mama said.
Eeh! My child, the *things* these eyes of mine
    have seen you can't believe.
Pthu! Pthu!

> *[She spat contemptuously on the hungry dry*
> *earth.*
> *I didn't say anything.*
> *I watched her spit swallowed by the earth.*
> *Then silence followed.*
> *Too much silence between us remained.*
> *I stole a glimpse of her saddened face.*

*A glint of tears formed at the corners of her
  eyes.]*

What? I said. What a sinister thing to say, Mama!

I know it is hard to believe such things, she said.

You know what our people believe? Mama added.

What? I said, as though I didn't know it already.

The dead usually have a way of marking their
  killers.

How so? I said.

When someone views a body laid in repose

And, let's say, the dead cries . . .

It is usually a sign! Mama said declaratively.

A sign? I said. Call me a skeptic about such
  things.

The dead always marks its killer, you know,

If the death were unnatural, Mama said.

My mouth went half-open in disbelief.

The skeptic in me doubted these words!

*[Yeah! Yeah! . . . I kept on thinking. The dead
  couldn't cry.*

*I had heard of it before, never thinking it came
  too close home.*

*If they did, maybe they weren't truly dead,
  but in a coma.*

*Yes, a coma made more sense. Perhaps, it
  was the youth in me,*

*which must have come in the way of me
  believing Mama.*

*So, I imagined many souls who might have
  been buried alive.*

> *Like the man near our village market who rose*
>   *from the dead!*
> *Lucky devil, it was only minutes before his*
>   *fate was sealed.*
> *What a tumult he caused. All the mourners*
>   *took flight.*
> *They planted a banana plant in his empty*
>   *grave to ward off bad luck.]*

That is how I *knew* she had killed my granddaughter.

That devil! Mama said and fell silent immediately.

What did you do when the corpse cried?

We chased Rosie out of your brother's home, she said.

> *[I broke into mirth,*
> *Wishing I had been there to bear witness.*
> *So, I imagined our sugarplum Rosie taking*
>   *flight,*
> *And funnily, with Mama in her pursuit.*
> *What a sight! What a delightful sight.]*

She didn't attend the funeral, Mama said.

Could you blame her? I said.

No, Mama said. It was for her own good.

I see, I said. I would have done the same.

Who knows what the village could have done to her!

Did Adonis come to the funeral? I said.

How could he? Mama said. He had met another,

Lucy Wambui, his bedfellow, and left Rosie to rot.

Really? I said, having never heard of Lucy.

Yes, Mama said. Rosie had become a relic of his
 past.

Poor thing, I said. Why didn't the village come to
 her rescue?

They couldn't, she said and became profoundly
 still.

Foolish men cannot be easily saved! That's the
 truth.

Uncle was not a foolish man, I said in protest.

You don't know men, Mama said.

No, you don't know him like I do.

True, I said. Maybe so!

He should have known better,
     Mama said.

Kipya kinyemi ingawa kidonda, she added.

Mama sometimes used Swahili proverbs,

None was more apt than this one,

A new thing can be a source of joy even if a sore!

True, I said, absorbing what Mama just said!
     [I learned it in school years ago,
     But I hadn't thought of it since then.
     I sat stalk still absorbing Mama's words.
     Aah! The absurdity of life!]

It took years for Adonis to learn this truth,
     Mama said.

I see, I said.

We buried your niece without incident, Mama
said.

With it, she added.

The village began to chip away at Rosie.

How unfortunate, I said.

You know the measure of a person is her deeds,
     Mama said.
What happened to Rosie after that? I said.
She remained unchanged, Mama said.
Really, I said.
Yes. She only clung to pieces of her past life,
     Mama said.
You must not tell anyone these things, she said.
Do you hear me? she added with seriousness.
     [I nodded my agreement,
     Even though this *was an open secret.]*
I didn't know if I should believe Mama,
     or doubt her words.
Could she have been lying to me?
That the Beautiful One had truly
Taken a life, my niece's life.
But how would she gain from it? I thought.
So, I let my mind recoil upon itself
     in reflection.
That is when an important saying
From our sages came back to me,
That 'The path of a liar is short!'
Clearly,
Mama couldn't spread falsehoods.
For 'Where there is smoke, there is fire!'
Certainly, hearing her story,
I knew there was too much smoke
     in her words to ignore!

After he left home,
Adonis did seldom come back,
But his visits were far in between,
Mostly during Christmas time.
And never lacked excuses for his absence!
Henceforth, the chasm of separation,
Unduly forced upon the two lovers,
Put a dent in their fledgling bond.
So, he rendered his intermittent services,
Whenever he chanced to visit her,
Fathering two lovely sons with her
Whose very tales are an eyesore to all.
Otherwise, he left her to her devices.

Mama said his absence was why Rosie,
The Beautiful One, became a village pariah.
To chase away her heart's loneliness,
Borne out of her husband's neglect,
She sought comfort from impious men,
Whose interest in her was never noble!
But she, being a cunning woman,
As cunning as a Satan,
Used her beauty charm
To arrest and tame men's hearts.
Yet, they hardly valued her!
Not her self-worth,
Not even her self-esteem,
She was nothing to speak of,
As useless as an airhead,

A mere plate of meat
To pacify their carnal desires.

❖

Thusly, Rosie's misdeeds went
     'unnoticed' for decades,
Even years after Adonis
Had returned home a pauper,
Even when he sank into depression,
And withdrew into alcoholism,
Nothing halted her waywardness.
If ever Adonis knew of it,
     no one knew.
Then,
When after a night-long drinking,
Guzzling *waragi* like at end of time,
He hobbled home like most drunks,
And tripped at his doorstep.
Too tipsy to gather himself up,
And fell into a deep slumber.

Then,
Right there, at his doorstep,
The unexpected happened.
The bowels of the sky opened,
As a storm of gigantic proportion
Fell and dealt him a punishing blow,
All night long until he expired.
Long before dawn.
Long before folks awakened.

Long before his brother's mournful,
And a piercing cry awakened the village.
Long before the sun had showered
Ngoroke with its luminous glow.
He vanished as though he never was.
Years after being laid to rest in gloom,
Rosie never stopped!
Not even a single flower, a rose
Was laid on his tombstone,
He, a scumbag unfit for tribute!

5

The Disgraced

Rosie, the Beautiful One,
Aptly named,
Weathered a lion's share of calamities,
Woes enough to last one's lifetime,
Though, Eliab's case exacerbated it all!
Too much misery for this daughter of woman,
That to craft a yarn to do her tale justice,
Of her unjust living, her bittersweet life,
Of her son's unexpected demise,
Gift from Adonis's loins,
Was a monumental endeavor.

Yes!
Adonis, her angelic husband that never was,
And undeserving of such accolade,
Had, left her sole bearer of the burdens
     of this loss,
Which birthed her mind's undue madness.
Any being, with heart, would have her grief felt.
But with her husband's neglect and absence
She had no one with whom to share
     this cup of bitterness,
Not even her meddlesome villagers
Whose tongues had soured against her,

Whose trumpet ears were forever open,
Taking in anything that floated their way—
The bad, the good, the ugly; all the chaff—
In the wake of their wakefulness,
           never letting up!
Whose watchful eyes, like sharp drills
Pierced her back, casting a dark shadow
Over her and sealed her fate in gloom.

Naturally then,
Her tested faith in marriage waned.
Who could blame her?
At least, not those levelheaded folks!

Yet,
Logooli sages often say,
Whomever sits on a throne,
Clinging onto the reins of power,
Up there on the pedestal of repute,
Trampling the little folks beneath their feet—
Unfit to cradle them with love and care—
Oblivious to their plight,
And without a care in the world,
In time, out of volition or force,
Their moment of descent into their reality,
Often arrives to them sooner than thought,
In youth, middle age, or old age!
They'll tumble down like a house of cards.
For such, was the case with Adonis,

Imali J. Abala

A man who had never thought,
From the crevices of his heart,
he would want for anything!

Yet,
When old age stroked his retirement,
At the ripe age of sixty-five, to be exact,
His time had marched on expectedly steadily!
As it must, Adonis,
Whose body had weathered
The ravages of time,
Was compelled to face the truth
      of his misdeeds!
He, a broken broke man returned home,
To his ancestral home of Ngoroke,
To a woman he had long forgotten.

Lucy Wambui, his second wife, and sons,
To whom he had given his all—
The syrupy sweet of his youthful honey—
Had the good man beguiled.
Tricked him to forgo his fortune,
The Title Deed of purchased land,
The only emblem of his retirement boon,
And cast him out of *his* home like garbage.

Empty-handed, his feet caked with dust,
And weather-stained, a hungry and tired Adonis,
Sadly, to his first wife, Rosie, he returned.

Like a prodigal son who had spent all his wealth
And begged for a father's mercy,
Adonis, did his forgiveness beg from Rosie,
Unaware as Mama's often said,
'Oyoya ovosera ni vusunduki ku kevooya mba!

[Mama's words, aptly stated,
Steeped in Logooli culture meant:
One must not cry over spilt milk.
It cannot be salvaged! Though,
Adonis aimed to give it his all,
Hopeful for tender mercies,
Recapture his long-lost love,
Extract the love notes he had on her heart
Engraved in his youth.]

The truth about Adonis' life
Was known to all in Ngoroke village,
An inscribed open secret,
For which all ate up like bread!
Rumourmongers knew it all—
The why and the how—
Most families in this good village,
Had, as a norm, sons who had left home.
Most returned, showering families with joy,
And most marvelled in the wisdom of sages,
That 'distance makes hearts grow fonder,'
But this did not come to pass for Adonis!
Distance did not make his heart grow fonder!

Imali J. Abala

The day he left home for city life,
Distance birthed a chasm between the lovers:
Rose, the Beautiful One, and Adonis.
Though, he might have claimed,
His surrendered heart wasn't the culprit for his fall,
But a desire to chase away his city loneliness.
Feeble of heart, and a *waragi* clouded mind,
He willingly discarded Rosie, the Beautiful One!
Being of sound mind and unforced,
He had yielded to Lucy Wambui,
Whose sweet-sounding words of love
Stroked the desires of his weak flesh.
So, he lost himself and scruples,
Of a wife's absence not meant to last.
And this, foolhardily,
Led to his lapsed memory,
His deceit for decades to come.
Lucy, like Samson's betrayer,
Delilah, tempered with his heart's frailty,
And when she duped him years later,
He sadly lost his life's locus and wife.

Alas,
A man whose voice had boomed his presence
Faded away like the passing wind,
As his actions rang his demerits in village life.
Now, he alone was left as a vagrant,
Floundering in his rags of poverty
That had birthed his exodus from home,
Chasing the fruits of promised *uhuru*,

Fruits meant to be won through sweat,
Not his sacrifice of family,
Unaware his body and heart's wants
            would give instead,
Than reap the spoils of his sweat.

So,
He lost his standing in society,
Becoming a mere beggar and petty thief.
Call it a case of abject humiliation!
No one could unmake this man,
As the regrets of his heart and garb
            lingered on to his end.
What a fair cry for the fallen!
For time, his time lost,
Was never recovered!
Who knew?

❖

Today,
Adonis is long gone!
Only Eliab is left to sneer a yarn of his life,
Detailing a series of his unfortunate incidents,
Of how he had sunk in the murk of disgrace,
Of how Lucy's ruthless hands
            had harp strummed his heart,
Like a strummed autoharp,
Ushering his lost humanity and defeat,
Mercilessly, she had milked his honey,
And struck him in his shrivelled balls!
Empty-handed, chased away like a dog,

And left broken-winged like a bird.
So, his cure— for mind, body, and soul—
Was as bleak as a moon's light
        on a cloudy night.

Barefooted and penniless,
He was chased out of his home.
As his feet slammed hard
        on a gravel-trodden path
As he sprinted in ire.
Merciless pebbles stabbed his soles,
In his flight and bled.
Pursued by his sons,
He huffed and puffed like an ass
Unduly forced to carry a burden
        too heavy to bear.
For the boys were oblivious to life,
He had for their living laid,
Unmindful of his daily sweat,
Come day or night, rain or shine,
Like his now sweat-soaked body
        in his flight for safety,
A sacrifice for which
        their comfort of living he met.
Now,
Their hearts of steel,
Twisted by a mother's lead heart,
Had turned against the very hands
That had fed them for decades.

Yet,
When he was miles away
From his *new* home,
The sons of woman,
With veiled threats of torture,
Forwent their chase,
But not before one,
Brandishing his fingers annoyingly
       in his direction said,
'As Nyasaye is witness,
Don't dare show your face here again,
Or else!'
'Or else what,' Adonis said.
'Your head, on a silver platter,
We shall to your,
Rosie, the Beautiful One, serve!'
      [Adonis never looked back.
      He ran home a wounded man.]
That is how Adonis,
A man, who could have won hearts,
Sank to the lowest times of his adult life,
As his heart sank in distress and knowing:
That as Nyasaye was his witness,
He had his old mat discarded for a new one!
Had Lucy's tongue, as of a shyster,
soured against him in a moments' rapture?
How had he not seen this brewing trouble?
Was he too blind to see her signs of betrayal?
Was this what happens to most men in *love*?

Imali J. Abala

Yesterday,
Without choice,
Adonis returned home broken,
Hoping to amend his ways,
With Rosie, the Beautiful One,
Change the tide of time,
Optimistic that he could reverse
The faults of youth in old age
Even if he would his flaws expose.
What a maniacal conundrum!
It seemed he had never heard of
'A stitch in time saves nine!'
For his he had at the seams ripped!

And so, yesterday,
When he was at his crossroads,
Adonis, an old and grey-haired man,
Must have swallowed his pride,
Or else his fall, he could've magnified.

Logooli folks believe in forgiveness.
For she or he who does not seek it,
Breaks the bridge upon which to pass!
It is a good antidote for the heart,
Builds character and for good living!
Yet, when one's heart is impaled,
Bringing healing to it is a nightmare,
A truth not far from Adonis' dilemma!

He hoped Rosie, the Beautiful One,
Would her heart soften upon his return,
Mend the bleeding scars of his betrayal!
For the virtue of forgiveness
Was no measure for the weak,
Save for those strong of mind!
Mama would, in all honesty,
Have agreed with Adonis' quest.
For to forgive was to love,
But without love, hate reigned.

Today,
After years of his absence, Eliab
With vividness, recalled it all,
That memorable day of Adonis' return:
A warm dry July morn
When the early dawn sun
Glistened like diamonds
Against the eastern sphere.
The emotive minute details of it
Enfolded in his present
Like a bloomed hibiscus,
Of Adonis' well-intentioned quest,
Securing his rightful place in a home,
Of decades-long forgotten
Unaware,
Dust settles thick on the forgotten,
Spinning tales too hard to dust off!

His unkempt appearance,
Like all things dishevelled,
Told his sad pathetic reentry,
Of his dirty torn clothes,
Of his swollen feet
From the stress of travel,
And caked with red dust,
Of the pungent smell of his body,
Too repulsive to invite an embrace!
And the white of his eyes,
Bloodshot and devilish,
Hardly warm and soft,
Birth fear rather than endearment!
Catlike, the brown of his pupils,
Sent chills to all those he met.

So,
It went without saying,
That Rosie, the Beautiful One,
Turned her nose away from him.
From the very man to whom,
Decades before this day in memory,
She had her heart willingly given.
She,
The noblest of his sweet-earned prize,
But broken by his betrayal,
For the stains of her yesteryears,
Were too deep to erase,
And swirled in her dizzying mind.
Left to face the Ngorokeans wrath

And rumourmongers alone,
Their tell-tales, enough to turn
A saint into a shrew!
Not shielded by his vow of love,
Oneness in spirit,
Not the jilting that later followed!

He had turned away from her,
Vanished from her midst like mist!
How could he then,
Suffering the impunity of his follies,
        expect manna?
Of the sweetness of her heart and love,
Which he let turn sour like milk in a gourd,
Rebuffed the very woman,
To whom he had promised glory,
But dropped a lump of coal in her lap!
Rosie, the Beautiful One,
Wasn't merciful to him upon his return,
As he had hoped for her warm embrace.

'Hell knows no fury,
Like a woman scorned!'
Some folks often say.
Who could blame Rosie?
Not even a single village trumpeter
Could blast her displeasure!
So, with Adonis' cold return
Distance between them widened,
As wide as the Indian Ocean.

Therefore,
Loneliness stroked his miserable life.
As Adonis took to mischief,
Raiding people's farms unashamed,
Reaping harvest from fields
To which he had not toiled,
And earned rebuke like Brer Rabbit
Caught in Mr. Fox's snare trap.
What a shameful act!
Yet, Adonis was no rabbit,
Neither was he caught stealing peanuts!
His exploits, he did with precision,
Often snuck into a neighbour's farm,
Dense with a thick maze of green,
Sprawled about him with foliage,
Overhanging leaves provided his shade,
A perfect concealer.
Slants of light often cast a shadow
Against his frail frame,
Which had weathered lashes of starvation.
Perched on his twos,
Wrapped his hands around an ear of maize,
And rabbit-like, nibbled at it!
He had not a single care in the world,
But he, *his* maize and Nyasaye.

When a neighbour nabbed him,
Caught him red-handed,
He broke into uncontrollable mirth!
Next to Adonis, right by his side,

Sat a calabash of raw maize,
Unhusked for his pleasure,
As his eyes,
Two glistening drills under the maize shade,
Darted back-and-forth, back-and-forth,
From the calabash to the maize
And back to the calabash.
The dark brown of his pupils, earth-toned,
Spoke of the heaviness of his untold past,
Of his loss and everything else
There was to a man's name,
And nothing more . . .

> *[What a rib-breaking yarn!*
> *My eyes were moist with tears,*
> *In disbelief in my hearing*
> *As Eliab spoke of Adonis'*
> *Fall from grace, of a man.*
> *Who once wore the garb of respect!]*

Adonis was oblivious to his foibles,
A brazen capture. Unafraid. Unashamed.
For he had become a new man,
A petty thief of raw maize and beans,
And *this* had become his legacy,
A hungry stomach knows no humility,
Neither does it know humiliation.
Aware of the hen that digs for food
Could never sleep hungry,
And he was that hen!
So, he embraced his failures as his norm.

When she got wind of Adonis' capture,
Rosie, the Beautiful One,
Gloated in his arrest,
And showed no mercy.
Much like a door of steel,
Which when opened
Shows no mercy to anyone!
Maybe, she was too old to care
About Adonis' antics.
So, she watched with glee,
As he was hauled to the *baraza*.
What a moment of disgrace!
There,
Under the great tent of blue sky,
Before a cold piercing gaze of all,
He silently accepted his penalty,
With the grace of a defeated man,
But remained unmoved by it!

Adonis had skipped out on time,
As though unaware,
Time, long lost, is forever!
For he had failed,
Like most foolish men do,
To cling onto this priceless gift,
Let it slip through his fingers,
Like worthless caustic potash,
Though vital for one's being.
Unfortunately, he showed no remorse
Unaware foolish deeds lead to regret,

But he made no effort
To mend Rosie's broken heart,
Not even reclaim bits of their lost time!

Thus,
Adonis' final days on earth,
With Rosie, the Beautiful One,
Were shrouded in gloom.
As their time, ghostlike,
Had passed them like the wind.
Then, nothing.
No sweetness caressed their hearts,
As both missed out on happiness,
Not even in a moment's rapture
For *their* time,
This elusive moment of bliss,
Was, to them, dead. Forever lost!

Eliab didn't mince his words,
When he told on his uncle
That Adonis and Rosie, the Beautiful One,
Were kindred of spirits,
Who loved and hated each other,
Bonded in the woes of their hearts,
Until death happily did them part!

6

The Hopeful Prisoner

Mama, our family matriarch,
Will honestly frown at me now,
For I am breaking her cardinal rule,
'Never to speak ill of others,'
For it is unbecoming and uncouth.
This is what Logooli people believe,
A mantra for stewardship to the whole,
And I couldn't agree more with her!

Yesterday, she told me,
'My daughter, listen to me,
Listen to what I am about to tell you!
My mother taught me these things.
She, too, was taught by her mother,
You hear? Never speak ill of others,
For no one is a saint, just human!'
As a dutiful girl, I nodded my agreement,
An affirmation of my obedience,
Call it my youthful bow to her order.

Yet today,
In the dimness of my mind
I can feel her disapproving eyes,
Gawking at me, piercing my back,

And knifelike, penetrating my flesh
      to the bone,
For I am about to tell on Rosie,
Aware I haven't crossed my life's river,
And I couldn't gloat at her drowning.
So, know that I don't mean her harm!

Yesterday, Rosie, the Beautiful One,
Traded her goodness for evil deeds,
Which, needlelike, entered her soul,
and spread like an oak tree in her village life.
As greed wrapped its gummy fingers
      around her brazen heart
Like her badge of dishonor, not honor,
Unaware her actions did maim and kill!

Pardon me Mama,
I cannot remain silent, not this time.
Whomever heard of truth being silenced?
It cannot be done.
It always finds a way out.
Truth be told, Mama,
Rosie's misdeeds are too vast to ignore.
Deservedly, not the measure of a woman
      who made hearts go gaga.
She could have been a saint, but she wasn't!
She, the unsaintly saint, did the innocent nab,
Flapping her wings of deceit and blinding all.
Only I, in the whole lot of Ngoroke,
Remains impartial in telling on her!

Come on now, bear this witness with me.
For these words fell off Eliab's lips,
My cousin who was no model citizen,
But a skimpy good-natured fellow,
Whom when his mind wasn't *waragi* dulled,
Would his jovial spirit make grumpy folks
Amongst us perk in joy and glee,
Uplifting our sorrowful souls.
Yet,
Eliab, feeble of heart,
Couldn't pacify his very own demons.
And, time, a file that works noiselessly,
Paved way for his fall from grace too.

Eliab's path, as he recalled it,
With Rosie, the Beautiful One,
Did cross, but it wasn't coincidental,
Call it a matter of familial affairs!
For Adonis, his father's brother,
Did his conniving smile touch
And beguiled Rosie, fating their meeting!
Like Adonis,
Eliab did fall into a stewpot of Rosie's fire.
He, like his uncle,
Fell for her foxiness,
And became outfoxed!

What was the problem?
You might ask. None whatsoever!
Profound beauty is never bad. Not at all.

Though, if misused, it spells trouble.
The Beautiful One did her beauty misuse,
And for her misgivings paid dearly!

> *[So, I thought—*
> *What would Mama have said about this?*
> *What do our people say about beauty?*
> *Perhaps, there is no beauty,*
> *But the beauty of action, skin deep,*
> *Not the rot that ruled Rosie's being.]*

Eliab, too, was never saintly,
But a gullible dimwit.
Waragi and gummy hands were his ruin,
For his love of money, man's oldest foe,
And often sharper than a sword,
Was his greatest downfall.

> *[How, might you ask?*
> *Allow me this short detour,*
> *Let me tell you!]*

Eliab desired no self-preservation,
Aware money was power and with it,
He was headed for heavenly bliss,
A life free from strife.
Stamping this ideal in his heart,
He dulled his senses and lost his self-worth,
Unaware true wealth is gained
Through hard labour, sweat and blood.
Come day or night, rain or shine,
Not stealing from the hand that fed him,

An act which landed him in the slammer,
But not before his pact with Rosie,
The Beautiful One was sealed in secrecy!
And this is how it came down . . .

Eliab Chanzu, Adonis' nephew,
Abandoned his all to Rosie, the Beautiful One.
He, a short petite fellow, a simpleton
A weakling of a man, without grit—
Mind, body, and soul—
And with every fibre of his being,
Was easily swayed like a reed on a windy day.

Though good-natured, calamity befell him,
Like an unhinged boulder from Maragoli hills
And smothered all his sensibilities.
With Rosie, the Beautiful One, at its helm,
He bore her unforgiving deliverance,
Of a raw deal so grotesque many cringed
Upon learning of it with sorrowful hearts.

So, he fell into her lap with the force of steel,
As she manipulated her way into his heart,
Whispering sweet words of religion in his ears.
That 'Son, trouble not your heart with sorrow.
Believe in Nyasaye. No, believe in me!'
I, in His honour, will do right by you,
Serve you in earnest and goodness,
For as long as I live now and forever
And as Nyasaye is my witness. Amen.'

'Being sound of mind,
I do hereby swear on my parents' graves,
To keep my word, my solemn promise to you
From today and for as long as I live,
That I will do you no harm.'
        [Eliab looked on,
        Muted and dumbfounded
        Ate Rosie's words like bread,
        Letting them permeate his soul,
        As though paralyzed by her utterances.]
Woe to Eliab!
Like a naïve starved knave,
Craving spiritual food,
He gobbled up her words,
Sighed and whimpered nonstop,
Like a lover blinded by love
A deep passion enough to drive,
A heart mad, as mad as hell!

Yet,
That was before he saw her true nature,
When he, son of woman,
Because of his impropriety,
Was cornered like a trapped rat,
Fell from grace, and plunged to hades,
Imprisoned for robbing his boss!

If only he had known . . .
That Rosie, the Beautiful One,
Whose smile tamed men's hearts,

Couldn't be trusted. Oh, dear!
How he could have saved himself
A lot of hurt,
Away from falling into purgatory,
To that point of no return,
Where only the strong survive,
Not for those easily beguiled,
Whose fear is the motherlode
Of their woeful sorrow!

The words of Rosie, the Beautiful One,
Were a snare from a woman scorned,
Whose tongue was as bitter as sap
From an Aloe Vera plant,
Too hard to swallow,
But believed to cure countless maladies.
Rosie, the Beautiful One, Eliab's antidote,
Sought to heal his self-inflicted wounds.
Yet, she led him to his very own damnation!
> *[Ngorokeans' ever-watchful eyes,*
> *Deep, penetrating, and inquisitive,*
> *That saw people's hearts, of darkness*
> *Seemed plunged into this darkness,*
> *Never heard of this insidious pact.*
> *And so, it went . . .]*
There, right by her side—
Rosie did his spirits perk
In love and in a sly tone,
Offered to guard his loot with all her being.
For she claimed as she massaged his heart,

'Son, trust me!' she had said to him.
'When you've done your time at Kodiaga,
Your cash will be still here, awaiting your return!'
> *[But this ill-gotten money*
> *Had trappings unseen,*
> *To good Ngorokeans folks.]*
Never thinking of anything,
Eliab, the innocent, agreed,
Sealing his fate in his blind trust,
In a being for whom no blood ties existed.
For genuine kindness in her words
> never existed,
But a foil to tame a gullible lad's heart,
Who was willing to trade his freedom
For the temporary high of stolen money.
> *[As Eliab unburdened his heart to me,*
> *My mind took flight to Mama!*
> *What could this old sage of mine say?*
> *What lesson would she have told him?*
> *Not much came to mind, but one,*
> *That money makes lies true,*
> *And it is a sure way to break bonds!]*
Thus,
Aunt and nephew colluded in their unholy union,
Though she wasn't in on the heist,
To which he alone was its architect—
Fraud was the nature of his heart—
As he was blind to one truth that . . .
Unjustly gained things are never permanent.

Like seasons—spring, summer, fall, winter—
They come and go like the wind.

For five years of his youthful life
Eliab sacrificed the comfort of home
          for his heart's greed,
And bore the whipping whips at a jailer's hands,
Which often lacerated his flesh nonstop.
Blood gushed out of his wounds like a spring,
And left uncountable rivers embossed on his back.
He didn't flinch in his torture,
But steadfast in his resolve remained
Aware the end truly justified his means.
Optimistic he remained certain
That the brokenness of his body was only,
But temporal!

In reticence,
He bore the brunt of prison life,
Of the stale smell of Kodiaga prison walls,
Of living in small jammed unlivable spaces,
And fed on food unfit for humans, but swine,
Lived amongst men whose crimes paled to his theft,
Those who had ended and defiled the sanctity of
   life,

Regrettably, men turned bestial!
Not to worry!
Eliab's perked spirit gloated in his awaited joys,
That rested beyond his sojourn in lock-up.

Full of knowing that he had wealth,
And, as Nyasaye was his witness,
He was cognizant of its power.
With this power massaging his mind,
He had no fear of prison life
            or its punishment.
Not even when the jailer's hands
Rained countless whips against his body.
Or when capricious men threatened him
With rape, the weapon of their choice!
He never waived, but knew his pain
In jail was merely a minor detour,
A guarantee of his pleasant years ahead!

Mama had once told me:
Time doesn't wait for anyone!
It doesn't slumber like a sheep in a pen.
Or humanity at a midnight snooze.
Time, she said, dissolves into itself—
At each dawning and dusking of the day—
It is ever there and unchangeable,
Yet once lost, it is unredeemable,
Just as was the case with Eliab.
Now,
Let me split open a crack into Eliab's mind,
For his time in prison came and passed quickly,
Like a tumultuous ocean breeze at a coastal
    shore.
The sun, steaming hot, rose and fell with his
    hope.

The moon, too, rose and fell with equal measure.
Seasons changed—the rainy and dry seasons—
But he remained hopeful and steadfast,
And counted minutes as they morphed into hours,
hours into days, days into weeks, weeks into
    months,
and months into years, he never tired!
For he knew of his awaiting dividends upon his
    return.

Nothing could have aroused his suspicion,
That he might have made a pact with the devil,
Or of the unholy folly in human hearts.
For he believed in Rosie, the ever-so-beautiful rose.
Whose tongue, he knew was as sweet as honey,
As its power wielded unyielding faith and trust,
A yardstick to scribe blind trust in Eliab's heart,
Of which his blissful future hinged, in her hands!
> *[Mama always told me, 'Child,*
>
> *There is no day that doesn't begin with dawn,*
> *Neither is there one that doesn't end with*
>   *dusk!*
> *And such is the nature of life. . .]*
Eliab's dawn came faster than he had thought.
When the doors of steel opened and closed
        behind him,
Releasing him from five years of his bondage,
Call it due justice for a crime committed in youth.
'Free at last! Free at last,' he must have thought,
Grinning from ear to ear with joy.

And yes,
The glee he now felt,
About this freedom was great,
No more euphoric than the truth
      of going home.
After a prison release,
Any being would have been joyful,
As joyful as a child in an ice cream parlor.
Bowing away from the spell of bad luck,
Of long-lost years, Eliab was about
      to clinch a blissful future,
Now within his reach,
Just as he had hoped and dreamed!

Therefore,
No sooner he set foot outside prison walls,
Than he dropped onto his knees and hands,
On a dew-covered earth.
With his eyes glistening with tears to the sky,
He blessed his ancestors for their protection,
And safety, from the beastly experience of prison,
Convinced they had not abandoned him!

All the while and for the first time,
He breathed in the fresh air of freedom,
Not the stale pungent prison smell,
But the sweet-scented floral spring blossoms,
Of scented plush stargazer lilies,
Jasmine, roses, and honeysuckles.
Aaah! Just divine.

In this moment,
The repugnant gas fumes of idling cars
And raving engines were divine!

Springing to his feet,
He took a calculated glaze at the prison walls,
As a choking lump crept into his throat.
He fought hard to tame his tears,
And dusted himself.
Then, without giving it much thought,
As the sun shone brilliantly in his eyes,
He took his first steps on his journey,
Home-bound at last!

The gait in his feet was light,
As light as that of a man walking on stilts,
Of measured steps,
Of a being whose destiny seemed assured.
And as he walked,
He listened to the thrums of his heart
          aware his dreadful past,
His woeful past was behind him now!
Time in the moment, was all he had left.
Yet, his future remained a mystery,
Hidden to all who know him in Ngoroke.

As he raced home,
To the pounding of his heart,
His eyes. Yes, his eyes shone fiercely like the sun.
But he experienced no his hidden fears,

Blinded to his sixth sense. No. No.
He had faith, real faith— selfless, profound!
Faith in the saintly Rosie, the Beautiful One,
Fully confident in their parting words . . .
A pact forged in secrecy and sworn:
'In my late mother's honour,' she had told him.
'I promise to guard your wealth!'

> *[Logooli's belief in a promise made honouring,*
> *Or in an invocation of the dead cannot be broken!*
> *Therein lay Eliab's conundrum!*

Her words were as good as gold,
Never once did he entertain obvious reality:
That truth can be stranger than lies,
And lies truer than espoused truth,
But soon, he would learn its biting sting.

> *[I wished I had been there,*
> *Right there in Ngoroke village,*
> *The very second of Eliab's grand entrance*
> *To the entranced trumpet ears of villagers!*
> *What a tale! That was not to be,*
> *Yet, to his tribute, I scroll this saga.]*

At the bus stop,
Eliab had wished he had wings to fly home,
It was not to be!
Instead, he was contended with a *matatu* ride.
Taking his steps into an idling van,
Its engine revved nonstop.
And sat down in wait, as the driver hooted

For passengers to fill empty seats.
Some did not bite the bait, but not many.
A twenty-minute wait seemed meagre
To his years of imprisonment,
A moment which was his measure,
To his awaiting peace of an excitable soul.

So,
He huffed and puffed his excitement,
And inhaled the fumes of freedom in stride.
Soon,
When the *matatu* filled up and smoothly glided off,
Grinding slowly against the black of the tarmac
  road,
Eliab's joy was as great as the joy
Of an excitable child at the sight of candy.
After paying his fare of twenty shillings,
He closed his eyes to a soothing cool breeze,
As it brushed gently against his sweaty brow.

As the van sped on,
He blocked off the ruckus sounds of riders,
But only awakened to the *matatu's* grinding tires
When the conductor alerted him of his stop.
His euphoria was immeasurable as he disembarked.
Yet, to get home, he still had a three-mile trek,
There was no *matatu* to ease the burden of this
  walking.
Therefore, he walked on . . .
No. He sprinted all the way home,

Ready to make a withdrawal of his deposit.

Rosie, the Beautiful One, was his bank,

From which he was certain still held the gains of
his joy.

No interest was necessary for her safekeeping.

His interest, her life and living!

7

The Beguiled

The afternoon of Eliab's home return,
Rosie, the Beautiful One,
Had been spotted lying on a mat
Under the shade of a jacaranda tree.
Its umbrella-like foliage
Sheltered her from the sun's piercing shards.
'What a beautiful afternoon!' she had thought.
A colossal infinite blue spread far and wide,
Below it, birds glided with ease to some unknown
    places.
Others, nestled amid tree leaves,
Chattered away noisily.
With her head cupped in the palms of her hands,
She closed her eyes and took in all these sounds.

So, when Eliab showed up,
She neither saw nor felt his appearance!
As his voice sounded a peace greeting, *Muleembe,*
He startled Rosie from her siesta
What a freaking shock . . .
The shock of a lifetime!
Amid the slumbering daze of her afternoon,
Rosie stirred from her dreamlike inertia
        to a horror image of her nephew—

Whom, for all intents and purposes,
Hoped for the warmth of her embrace,
Not the loud ear-shattering scream—
Like of a woman in fear for her life,
A kind of dirge one sounds when a home
        is visited upon by death—
Perhaps, she had every reason to be fearful.
Eliab, unamused, was taken aback,
Yet, he was interested only in one thing,
To collect the dividends for his due sacrifice,
Of which Rosie, the Beautiful One,
Had vowed to safeguard with her life,
Unaware, their pact had nearly cost her life,
Demonized by his kinfolk for it,
Giving her unwarranted grief,
Demanding his very every cent!

'What do you want?' was all she could say,
Not soothing words, 'Welcome home, son!'
Recalling the agony she endured from his folks
Who wanted to skin her alive.
With those sad four simple words, the Beautiful
One,
Had, without his regard, shattered a life into
    pieces,
A million unrecoverable and unpeaceable pieces,
Like a miserable and worthless dog.
She had expelled him from her home penniless.
'Get the hell out of my home,' she bellowed!
Thus, their pact sealed in secrecy imploded,
As the village bore witness and for their delight.

Immediately, madness, real madness,
Became Eliab's presence and stroked his heart.
How was he to explain himself?
The village had heard and started gossiping,
Unaware gossiping is the devil's radio!
Mama couldn't and wouldn't believe it.
That the Beautiful One had, without care,
Her nephew mercilessly beguiled!
How had he missed her signs?
Mama had, in years past, not paid real attention,
When the Beautiful One suddenly fell
        into good fortune.
No one did. No one questioned.
No one knew it. Not even the village mongers,
Of how Rosie could, after Eliab vanishing,
Afford her flamboyant living,
Not her familiar life of strife
Much like all Ngorokean.
But with her husband in the city,
Most folks assumed Adonis had,
In his late father's honour,
Come to his senses by remembering his wife.
Making the rumour mill go mum on this one,
As quiet as dawn!

Yet,
When Beautiful One shunned Eliab,
She exposed their secret pact,
That had laid hidden and dormant for years,
Slumbered in people's suspicious memory,

Like a slumbering lion!
Yet now, it flew open,
Exposing Rosie for who she was,
The dirty rotten scoundrel of Ngoroke,
A scum artist who destroyed others in a blink.
Not even a penny did Eliab get for all his pain,
Of countless marks of torture embossed on his
    back,
An emblem of his youthful errors!

Decades have come and gone,
Since then, but to this day,
The dread that followed Eliab's shaming
Has remained stamped on people's minds.

> *[Mama often spoke of Forgiveness that:*
> *One who offends another must ask for a*
>   *pardon,*
> *But for the offended, forgiveness is*
>   *essential.*
> *I couldn't agree more with her,*
> *But for Eliab, it wasn't clear cut!]*

Eliab's return home was marred,
With a series of unfortunate events!
Penniless and unemployed,
Years of his prison life as a legacy marked him,
A legacy he couldn't escape.
As an untouchable man,
He took to *waragi* and dulled his senses.
For he had no one with whom to share
    his cup of bitterness.

Sometimes though,
Nyasaye's mercy is greater than man's.
For no sooner had love fallen in his lap,
Than Eliab thanked Him for his good fortune.
A love to which he clung, eyes and mind closed.
Perhaps he, too, stood a chance at happiness,
Though he couldn't forget his past.
This love was a reminder of honey sweetness,
And often joked, 'Even those ugly of heart,
Do eventually find true love.
I couldn't forever wallow in sadness!'

8

The Devil's Radio

How can I play a flute in praise of Rosie,
The Beautiful One, if her song is wicked?
For I cannot find the tongue to make merry
      in her honour,
Neither can I find sweet words,
To memorialize her in the Book of Life
Save to only sing a nursery rhyme,
Mama sang to me when I was a little girl,
Of how Logooli folks 'cured' mumps:
      Ndendeyi hera ku umuteembe
      Ndendeyi hera ku umuteembe
      (Mumps remain on *umuteembe* tree)
So, with it,
I seek to ward off Rosie's unleashed
      rivers of bad luck,
She transformed, much like mumps,
If left unscathed might do others harm?
Would she run around *umuteembe* tree,
The way children did, back in the day,
To ward off bad luck from the village?
I couldn't vouch for this outcome!

Though, sadly,
I know Mama was dead wrong,

To toot in Rosie's defence.
To disregard her misdeeds
Would be a miscarriage of justice!

So, I know Mama might have a fit,
Of me telling on Rosie again.
Of course, she would say,
'Some tales need no telling.
They ought to be left in the annals of history,
Especially if ill-gotten and yarned
           out of ill intention.'
Of course, she might be right,
Though, I don't mean Rosie any harm.
Folks with impure thoughts,
Folks who attract bad energy,
Folks whose actions are ever-changeless,
Who never care whom they hurt,
Who never bear in mind a sage's advice,
I say, 'Once bitten twice shy!'
For an axe forgets, but a tree remembers.
Thus, when pushed to the limit,
Any person is bound to retaliate,
An act of revenge borne out of a rush,
An adrenalin rush to save or protect the self,
Lest the victim forever live in shame.
And such was the case with Eliab,
Who sought to stamp out *zindendeyi,*
The very root cause of all his troubles!

❖

Eliab's story, I must admit,
Deserves a double-take, not a blackout.
That is what Mama would expect of me,
Blackout Eliab's entire tale.

True, for some folks,
Their lives are always riddled with misery,
Forever in crisis!
Perhaps, you might know such a person.
And that no matter what they do,
No matter the circumstances of their lives,
They always make their very situations worse.
And Eliab was no stranger to this!
Bad luck followed him with each turn he took!

Most people in the village could argue,
That he hadn't had many rainbows in his entire
    life,
Having been born into a family without riches,
And lived in a small grass-thatched mud house.
Hence darkness seemed to loom in his present.
That is why I've chosen to devote a few lines,
In my rumblings, to jot his bad-good life!
Of a life lived in disharmony, not harmony!

When Eliab found love—
        Andeyo Midecha—
And she conceived,
He saw a ray of hope on his faded horizon,
She became *the* rainbow of his adult life,

A harbinger of his good fortune.
So, he held his head high like a man,
Who, in the spur of the moment,
Had won a monumental lottery,
For which only goodness emerged!

Nonetheless,
His elation was as short-lived,
As is the case when a sudden fortune
Befalls those less fortunate.
Much like his earlier dream of loot, of glory,
A boon which had landed him in prison.
 I say, 'Easy come, easy go!'
Soon became a hallmark of his life.

When Andeyo got pregnant,
Months into their relationship,
He proposed and pledged to bestow her honour,
A well-intentioned plan and as expected.
For fatherhood was his coveted dream.
Being a husband was his other desire.
Thus, his natural duties were mapped,
Precluded by societal norms.
Nothing out of the ordinary.

Since life is never predictable,
On one sunny morning,
As he readied to execute his plans,
A strange thing happened,

Maybe not so strange, but to him,
It altered the very course of his life!

Sadly, Andeyo lost their baby unexpectedly.
What a twist of fate to occur that fateful morn.
For Eliab's day erupted in dread and gloom,
As he witnessed his intended, angel of his heart,
Writhing in pain and cradling her fat belly,
 As she cried her heart out without relief,
And he felt paralyzed by this turn of events,
Utterly unable to share in her bitter cup of pain.
Caught betwixt finding a wheelbarrow
To wheel her to a clinic or carry her on his back,
And Boom! Everything fell apart in a twinkling.
For he saw streaks of red snake down her thighs,
Birthing the couple's terrible loss and misery.
This very child lost in a moment's rupture,
Had seemed the hope for Eliab's adult life,
Meant to give him meaning and purpose,
Or serve as a calming effect on his life of strife,
A child who had been there just for a while,
A tangible being, yet now intangible,
And had now faded away into the sunset,
Like mist on a sunny morn and never to be!

Today,
Eliab, a sad lonely man,
Is left to face fate, his impunity.
Although not on that fateful day.

Then, he cursed a storm all day long,
For misfortune had visited him, yet again.
Self-pity and self-loathing settled in his heart,
Like the giant rocks that dot the Ngoroke terrain.
In this moment of deep sorrow,
He recalled *the curse,*
An unforgettable curse that had
      the makings of something awful.
Rosie's magnificent reward to Eliab,
When he demanded his dues from his theft,
She, freakishly, cursed him!
Her words are carved on his gaping heart,
Like the scars of his prison life,
That is forever imprinted on his back,
Words that still haunt him now
That she, allegedly, claimed,
Were borne out of his disrespect for her!
'I guarantee you, mark my words,
You'll regret this for the rest of your life!
For your future success, to ward off *this* ill luck,
Much like a child inflicted with *zindendeyi*
Runs around a tree to ward off bad luck,
You must have your way with me!'
And Rosie meant every word of it!

What a blasphemy—
An outrageous proposal,
Such a thing has never happened!
Ngorokean villagers would,
In honour of their spiritual ancestors,

Who often spoke of *mileembe* – peace
As their mantra of everyday living,
Throw a fit and detest it as an evil act,
A crime for which one could take a life.
How could Eliab, Rosie's nephew,
Son of her brother-in-law,
Have his way with this 'devilish' woman?
What a taboo of gigantic proportion!

At first,
Eliab dismissed Rosie's words as a mere rant
          of a woman at her wit's end,
Aiming to even uneven scores,
Justified or unjustified,
To deflect the heat off her misdeed—
Robbing the poor fellow blind.
Though Eliab, as a superstitious man,
Gobbled Rosie's words like one eats food,
Doubting if there was truth to them.

This changed after Andeyo's miscarriage.
That was a sign of Rosie's power over him.
What black magic could she have used?
For words have the power to build or destroy.
Hers were not meant in kind and couldn't be,
Though kindness was all Eliab could have used.
Henceforth, his life, like before,
Spiralled out of control,
As he and *waragi* became pals again!
What a terrible bloody mess!

Before long, Andeyo left him,
To whom his heart he had surrendered,
Abandoned him with swiftness,
Like one abandons meat gone rancid.
Then, with the same swiftness,
Darkness fell upon his soul, yet again!

Yesterday—
Eliab visited me again!
It was in the early morning hours,
A broken dishevelled man he was!
Tears ran down his cheeks like a river.
His eyes, red hot like sizzling embers,
Spoke the grief of his sorrowful heart.
His loose lips seemed eager to flap
His mind and to disburden his grief,
Whatever it was that bedevilled him,
And had brought him to my midst.

Therefore,
I sat by his side in muteness,
Under the shade of our jacaranda tree,
And the sun rose above Maragoli hills
I was ready to eat up all his words,
Syllable by syllable, details of his vile life,
At least so I thought convinced,
A man's dignity resides in his given word!
      [Mama, I could never fib,
        Not about Eliab's story! Our people say,
        Each river has its own source!

For Eliab is the true source of his tale,
No one else, as Nyasaye is a witness.
No need to chastise me for this!]

My sister! Eliab said,
Let me tell you something!
Tell me what? I said.
Rosie has done it again!
Done what? I said.
Killed her neighbour's wife, he said.

> *[I took a minute to absorb*
> *The weight of his words.*
> *The sun was now sizzling hot,*
> *And peaked above Maragoli Hills.*
> *Eliab's uncontrollable heart beat his hurt.*
> *For I'd thought the chatter of murder*
> *Was merely a fabrication, not grounded in*
> *truth,*
> *But I decided best to humour my guest's*
> *theory.]*

How did she do it? I said.

> *[Quick to speak, Eliab's tongue,*
> *As bitter as bile,*
> *Riled its venomous sting against Rosie.]*

The Beautiful One's conniving antics had,
This time, another was implicated, he said.
For she had sweet-talked a servant girl
to steal ashes from her neighbour's kitchen.

> *[Eliab was such a superstitious man!]*

How do you know that? I said.

Don't you know the village has eyes and ears?
  he said.

I know that! I said.

Truthfully, the girl told me, he said.

She was her associate.

Who is this girl? I said. My curiosity piqued.

I cannot tell you that, he said.

What did Rosie do with the ashes? I said.

She used black magic to further her end? he said.

How? I said.

When she got possession of the ashes, he said.

> *[He paused, weighing his next words.*
> *Maybe it was the frown on my face,*
> *Which had driven him to silence.]*

She had her will done, he said!

What was her will? I said.

To snuff her neighbour's wife's life, he said.

I see. Any proof of that? I said.

She is dead, isn't she? he said.

Of course, she is dead, I said.

That's why she collapsed,

Under the spell of Rosie's witchcraft! he said.

No doctor's hand could have

Reeled her back to life, he added.

Are you sure about that? I said.

Rosie cut her life short unjustly!

Eliab said with sadness.

Why do you think she killed her? I said.

I don't know. Malice knows no boundaries,
  he said.

[If Eliab's slander of Rosie were true,
It went beyond a tangled web of deceit.
It was a truth with deep tentacles,
Beyond the land of the living.]

Areyo appeared to me in a dream, he said.
With her body, swaddled in sparkling white,
She had come to 'tell on' Rosie, expose her!
Oh! Really? I said.
Yes, expose her true nature, he said.
I can still see her now! he added.
Are you sure about this, I said.
Yes, I can still see her in my mind's eye, he said.
Especially her eyes . . . Those large brown eyes,
Like the earthen hue under which she is laid.
She showed urgency in her mission.
What was her mission, I said.
To put a stop to Rosie before she killed again!

> *[Eliab had trouble keeping details straight,*
> *As the rivers in his eyes ran down his cheeks,*
> *Forcing his silence. I looked on.*
> *He sniffled the sorrows of his heart*
> > *for a while. I let him be.*
> *Then slowly but surely, he reached out*
> *For one of the sleeves of his blue tattered*
> *And unwashed t-shirt and wiped dry his*
> > *face.]*

Why is that?
I asked him, confused by his proclamation.

> *[Eliab remained speechless.*
> *And I, like a mute, looked on for a while.]*

What do you plan to do? I said

After a searing moment had elapsed.

I am telling on her! he said.

That's what I plan to do.

What good would that do? I said.

> *[He didn't say anything.*
>
> *Maybe, there was nothing to say.*
>
> *I kept my eyes fixed on him.*
>
> *He didn't flinch, not even once.*
>
> *As I looked into his eyes,*
>
> *eyeball-to-eyeball, in I saw a glitter of tears.*
>
> *Instantly, I sensed the import of his mission.*
>
> *Like Mama often said in facing a challenge,*
>
> *As Eliab's case, 'There is no smoke without fire.'*
>
> *For sure, in Eliab's eyes, I saw too much smoke.]*

Just then, I heard her voice, Mama's voice,

For it was from the land beyond the living,

A cautionary voice, a whisper in my ear,

'Areyo died of a stroke!' That is what I knew.

I shook my head to silence her voice,

But she was relentless.

'Child,' Mama said again,

'Areyo died of a stroke!'

> *[Rumors often are the Devil's radio!*
>
> *Could Eliab or the village be the Devil?*
>
> *Who could trust the village trumpeters?*
>
> *Yet, in my mind, Eliab's voice*

> *Overshadowed Mama's cautionary voice,*
>
> *For he couldn't halt his slanderous tongue.]*

The Beautiful One killed *my* Areyo, Eliab raved.

Do you have proof? I asked.

She didn't attend her funeral, he said.

How is that proof? I said.

She was afraid of being exposed, he said.

How so? I said.

The dead have a way of telling on the living, he said.

I see, I said.

They have a way of marking

Those who did them harm, he said.

> *[Suddenly, I recalled Mama's story,*
>
> *What she said about my niece's death.*
>
> *Her corpse cried when Rosie came to view it.*
>
> *She was a no-show at her funeral,*
>
> *Which was deemed a community affair.*
>
> *Villagers came to their natural conclusion,*
>
> *That Rosie had had a hand in her death!]*

What did she say in her defence? I asked.

Nothing! What could she say? Eliab said.

> *[The rumour was that Rosie was very ill.*
>
> *That is what the village trumpeters said.*
>
> *It was a matter of conscience in tumult,*
>
> *But no one could confirm this truth.]*

Not long after Areyo was laid to rest, Rosie,

The Beautiful One was seen at her home,

   Eliab said.

Some people said she was after her husband.

With Areyo dead, Eliab added.

Rosie was her natural replacement!

Couldn't she have been simply being neighbourly?
I said.

Nope! Eliab affirmatively disagreed.

I shrug my shoulders at this rumour,

An insidious slander for a woman,

Whom, if she had been present,

She might have defended herself,

Not on this day,

She had no way to protect herself.

> *[Eliab dropped his head to the ground.*
>
> *His body looked like a question mark.*
>
> *I wondered what he must be thinking.*
>
> *Dark clouds glided above us like giant cotton balls.*
>
> *A pregnant moment of silence elapsed.*
>
> *He sniffled softly as mounting fury grew within him.*
>
> *When he finally spoke again, his words were chocked,*
>
> *As rage ran through his veins like venom!]*

As though Areyo's death had opened Eliab's mind,

He said with clenched teeth,

I know her other secret you don't know.

> *[He clasped his fingers together,*
>
> *And rubbed them vigorously.*
>
> *He didn't mutter a word for minutes.*
>
> *I closed my eyes in this silence save for my mind.*

It raced a thousand miles.
I tried to recall Rosie's secret,
But my mind was blank,
As blank as the face of a blind man.
When he spoke his truth,
Nothing could have prepared me for it.
The words that fell off his lips,
Honest and sincere words,
Carried with it the weight of slander,
Of gigantic proportion!]
Let me tell you, he said!
If you do not believe me, ask my nephew.
He will tell you the truth.
Nyasaye's Truth as I am about to tell you.
What did she do this time? I said.
What could she have done,
That is greater than murder?
[By then, Eliab had my attention.
I opened my eyes at this pronouncement.
Could there be anything greater than murder?]
Well, he said, you be the judge!
I am merely a vessel in its delivery.
The tale below is what he said . . .

9

When Truth Trump Fiction

Yesterday,
When Eliab came to see me,
He was heavy of heart,
As its burdens seemed,
Greater than the wage
Of the sin it carried.
That mid-morning hour,
The brilliant sun's fingers
Were spread wide above the hill
And glowed like molten iron.

When he made this appearance,
He looked scruffy and muddy.
What a sight he was!
It seemed he and Trenches,
Had been bedfellows.
His brown pants,
Torn by the knees,
Were grass-stained,
And muddy like his mud-caked feet!
Perhaps, he hadn't bathed in days.
Whilst his blue T-shirt
Had an inscription that read:
  'Wild about vision.'

His eyes, as red as coal,
Bulged with a seething fury,
Of unstoppable vengeance.
And his mind dulled with *waragi,*
Carried with it the weight
Of suspicion against Rosie.
His breath,
The smell of a brewery,
Too toxic to a nondrinker,
Was pungent,
Enough to make an abstainer drank,
Even if only by association!

On that day,
Eliab unburdened his heart to me,
Of what ensued after Adonis was laid to rest.
That his wife,
Rosie, the Beautiful One,
Had committed a vile crime,
An unpardonable immoral act
The sin of the flesh
Against her own,
Flesh of her flesh.
It was the kind Mama,
Our moral guardian,
Would have disdained.
Truly,
Without knowing *it,*
I wasn't shocked by the news.
No one was free from sin!

Mama often said,
By virtue of being born,
Weren't we all sinners?
By virtue of being human,
Weren't we all sinners?
Sane of mind,
I couldn't agree more with her.
I couldn't cast my stone against
Rosie, the Beautiful One, for her sins.

Thusly,
I couldn't tell if Eliab's words
Weren't insidious rumours
From a Devil's spun radio aimed at her.
> *[I listened to him with rapt curiosity,*
> *Wondering about the vile crime*
> *She must have committed to rile Eliab,*
> *Whom we all knew was a pacificist by nature.*
> *My doubts were laid to rest the moment*
> *Eliab disclosed to me of her sin, atrocity.]*
There was nothing to tame his burning fury,
A volcanic rage.
A rage about to erupt like hot lava
When it shoots through its conduits!
So, I looked on in silence,
Bewildered by his mere physical appearance.

What's wrong Eliab? I said to him.
I – I – I, he said, his words choked,
As though he couldn't find his tongue.

What's the matter? I said.
He poised himself but remained soundless.
I reached out and tapped his shoulder.
His body quivered to my touch,
Reminding me of a mimosa plant
That recoils itself to a human touch.
Momentarily,
He broke down into tears,
That ran down his face like a stream,
But wiped not his cheeks nor eyes,
And sniffled nonstop.

So, I grabbed him by the hand,
Hoping to lead him to a shade.
Unwilling to move,
He dragged his feet
Like an overworked ass.
No. An old man
Whose energy was already spent.
Once there,
He dropped his bottom
Onto a bench under the shade like a log.
It creaked noisily under his weight.
Yet, still muted,
Eliab's tongue seemed too heavy
To express the sorrows of his heart.
He lowered his eyes to the ground,
As his tears, two icicled rivers,
Drop-by-drop,
Fell onto the grass,

And glistened in the sun.
A moment of silence elapsed.
I am so mad, he said.
> *[His eyes, two bulging,*
> *Red drills were still on the ground.]*

Why is that? I asked.
The Beautiful One! he said.
That's who!
My heart sank at his pronunciation.
What's wrong with her, I said.
It is not what is wrong with her! he said.
It is what she did?
> *[Once more, my heart sank,*
> *Wondering if she had killed again.]*

What has she done this time? I said.
She . . . she has . . . has done a bad thing.
No. A very evil thing! he added.
What is *it* this time? I said again.
> *[By this time, I was getting frustrated!*
> *Why couldn't Eliab name it faster,*
> *Whatever the 'it' was?*
> *I was ready to receive it.]*

A vile sin! he said.
A sin? I said. Haven't we all sinned?
No . . . No! he said.
A sin. I mean a very . . . very big bad sin!
> *[I looked at him befuddled.*
> *Beads of tears formed in his eyes again,*
> *And fell onto the ground.*

> *I watched them dissolve into the dry
> hungry earth,*
>
> *And until a patch of moist brown formed.*
>
> *I raised my eyes and looked up,*
>
> *The sun's blazing beams showered the
> skyline.]*

What do you mean? I said.

The sin of the flesh, he said.

Too blasphemous to mention.

Oh! I said. The sin of the flesh isn't strange.

Many folks have fallen victim to it!

> *[Eliab fell soundless, but my thoughts
> raced.*
>
> *I wondered, if a sin of the flesh was a
> crime,*
>
> *Or was it?*
>
> *Could Eliab be fibbing against Rosie?*
>
> *Hadn't the villagers cast a wide net for her
> faults?]*

Save for murder, I said.

The sin of the flesh isn't so bad.

You don't *understand*, he said.

Did she kill someone, I said.

No, he said.

Did she steal or bear a false witness? I said.

Maybe against her neighbour?

Not that kind of sin, Eliab said.

If not, then what kind? I said.

Make me *understand!*

To live again after Adonis' death, he said,

She had to reclaim the urges of her flesh!

As a norm, she had to cut *ilikoola*
        –banana fibre!
Why is that a sin or a bad thing? I said.
Haven't we all sinned?
Haven't we all fallen short of Nyasaye's glory?
No. Aren't all humans sinners? I ranted.
You don't get it! he said.
Make me, I said.
It was with whom she chose
To render the service
Which is evil . . .
A form of debauchery, he said.
Whom did she choose? I said.
Her grandson!
Woi! Woi! What? I said.
        [Befuddled, I thought my ears
        Had betrayed me in my listening.]
Yes, her son's oldest boy, he said.
The one who died a while back.
What in heaven's name? I said.
What made her do that?
Lord have mercy on us!
Aah! Yap, she surely did,
Eliab said affirmatively.
Only Nyasaye can have mercy
On her wretched soul, he added.
How do you know this? I said.
        [Right then, all energy in my body felt spent.
        Eliab fell silent, as silent as my thoughts.

I couldn't draw words off his lips fast enough.

But when his lips parted in speech,

I understood the meaning of his distress.]

The boy's teacher told on her, he said.

How did the teacher know? I said.

The boy went to school days

      after his grandfather's burial.

And did he tell them this? I said.

No. He was walking funnily, he said.

What does that mean? I said.

He wobbled about like a duck, he said.

A duck? I said. That's a first . . . and?

The teacher sent him to the clinic for a check-up.

From walking like a duck? I said.

That sounds too far-fetched, I added.

Yeap! he said. That was *the* clue.

What happened then? I said.

The nurse called the teacher, he said.

The boy was still at the clinic at the time.

[Eliab fell silent again.

I didn't probe him with questions.

I wanted to . . . really,

But a look at him made me stop.

An ocean formed in his eyes,

But his nose ran like a stream.

After allowing a moment's lapse,

I pressed him on it for details.]

What did the nurse say? I said

His manhood was bruised.

Really? I said in disbelief.

What caused the boy's injury?
He claimed his grandmother
          forced him to have sex with her.
Holy crap! I said.
What kind of world do we live in?
Poor boy!
He was still a virgin, he said.
          [I was astonished beyond belief.]
Some nitwits had told her to do it, he said.
What for? I said, seething with rage.
I already told you why, he said.
She had to cut *ilikoola.*
I see! What did the teacher do? I said.
The teacher called the chief,
Who came right away, Eliab said.
          [Still dumbfounded,
          I said nothing for a while,
          processing the news, of which
          I hoped never to hear again.]
When questioned, Eliab said.
Rosie claimed the boy lied.
That is what the boy said, Eliab added.
I am not fibbing, he pressed on.
No one can lie about that, he said.
I see, I said.
Particularly, not against a grandmother, he said.
If I am lying, may lightning strike me!
Look here! he said with seriousness.
If you don't believe me,
Well, that is your problem!

[Silence fell between us and remained,

But when I found my tongue,

Only three words came out!]

Eliab, I said. That's scandalous!

Pure blasphemy, Eliab added.

[Who could believe a mere boy's truth

Over the Beautiful One's plea of innocence,

A woman whose eyes turned hearts,

And made men tremble in her midst?]

Do you know the rotten part of it? Eliab said.

No. What? I said.

She has a thing in for me now.

Wololo! I said. She has gone mad.

No. The world has gone mad.

Indeed! he said.

Why, I said.

I don't know, he said.

What do you mean? I said.

She wants me to *do* her too . . .

[I shook my head in disbelieve]

That is,

If I ever want to have children!

What in heaven's name

Are you talking about?

My gospel truth, he said.

I am telling you she did!

Lord have mercy, I said.

And why is that?

I *know* she is the reason

Areyo lost our baby, he said angrily.

My goodness, I said.

When did she become *the* goddess of fertility?

I don't know, he mumbled his response.

You must be truly mistaken, I said.

No, he said. As Nyasaye is my witness!

Don't take Nyasaye's name in vain, I said.

I thought she had fibroids, I said.

Nope, he said.

Didn't they say her mother said it?

Nope. Not true. You are wrong.

> *[Having nothing to add,*
> *I looked on, absorbing the news.]*

Let me tell you another, he said.

The Beautiful One herself told me.

What? I said.

She did and I believe her! he said.

Holy mother of God! I said.

Wake up, my brother.

Fibroids can cause a miscarriage.

I *know* what I am talking about, he said,
> stressing the word *know*.

For the love of peace and your sanity, I said.

Get your head out of the gutter of blame.

Stop listening to the noisy village chatter.

You do not understand, he said.

Such things happen to some women, I said.

> *[Eliab did not and could not listen.*
> *How could he?]*

Rosie told me herself . . .

That she put a curse on me, Eliab said.

If I don't have my way with her,

I am doomed. She can't lift her curse!

For your own sake, I said.

Don't listen to her foolishness!

> *[I looked at Eliab in disbelief.*
>
> *No. I was too stunned!*
>
> *I didn't know if I ought to believe him.*
>
> *What a bizarre tale, stranger than fiction!*
>
> *If the Beautiful One's words were a curse,*
>
> *Weren't they veiled hints of a troubled mind?*
>
> *How could Rosie bring so much harm to others?*
>
> *Eliab, that is! Where was Nyasaye to his rescue?]*

I tell you, Eliab said.

I don't intend to oblige her request.

I hope not, I said.

I would rather die in shame, he said.

Than degrade myself that way.

I couldn't agree more, I said.

I'd rather tie a noose around my neck, he said.

Don't be too dramatic, I said.

I am not. It is the truth, he said.

> *[I believed him. The part of taking his life.*
>
> *Eliab was just crazy enough to take his life.]*

I cannot drink out of my uncle's cup, Eliab said.

Aha! I said. I hear you. Such nobility!

I'll be the first one to come and whack you!

I am ready to wear my dignity to my grave, he said.
I see! I said. You better. For as long as you live.
Whatever dignity I still have left of it, he said.
I am certain Mama will approve of your resolve!

He didn't say anything else after that.
Maybe there was nothing to be said.
His message was delivered,
As loud and clear as a horn.

Then,
Silence fell between us and remained.
We sat as still as steel posts for a long time.
In our silence, we watched time pass by.
We hardly noticed the sun rising to its zenith.
Or when it faded away hours later
          against the azure sky.
I imagined the riotous activity
On his mind, of revenge! Aah!
The sweet smell of revenge
Especially, of a sick sane mind.
Amid it all, though,
I wondered if he knew the wages of revenge.
That he who seeks to do others harm
Unwittingly might harm himself.
That revenge is a fool's paradise,
And not for the wise!
Mama would have said,
Revenge is never good,
It turns a little right into a giant wrong!

When darkness fell hours later,
Against our Ngoroke village,
Eliab took leave for his home,
Having made *peace* within his heart . . .
That he alone would drain Ngoroke's swamp.

For he had resolved that:
Rosie, the Beautiful One,
Who truly never was,
Would never wreak havoc on society again.
That he alone, the ultimate avenger,
Would, by the might of his hand,
Render cold justice to avenge her victims.

That night,
When he left my home,
Darkness shrouded him along his way.
As he walked into the womb of the universe,
His life's mission was as clear as day,
Determined never to strum the strings
Of his harp in honor of the fallen angel.
The vanquished deserve no song,
   Save for scorn!

Meanwhile,
I remained in the darkness of my heart,
Wondering if he was right.
That Rosie, the Beautiful One,
Was truly an evil woman,
A devil in human clothing,

Whose steel-belted heart
Exploited the innocent for thrills.

That is the poetry of a woman,
Whose life was lived in disharmony,
Who sits on her front porch,
With her large brooding brown eyes to the sky.
While her heart, a sea of sorrow,
Seemed untouched by the slanderous
Words of those whose bitter tongues
Had not left her unscathed.

Now, at the young age, of seventy,
The Beautiful One had withered plenty,
Like a leaf under the sun's smouldering heat,
But age hadn't improved her being,
It had simply toughened her heart.
Neither had the village changed its view of her.
For she was still a meddlesome saintly devil,
Left alone to nurse her bruised ego,
And the depravity of her lived existence,
Yet again, newly accused.
Soon, and only too soon,
Her end, as gloomy as a moonless sky,
Lurked on her horizon, her avenger,
Clothed in human form,
Skulked in darkness, wielding a machete,
To execute his vengeance.
True cold justice!

10

The Devil's Own

Call me naïve,
But I believe Mama was right.
That evil folks exist in this world,
They come to us in many forms,
Some dressed in suits and dresses—
Some are kings and queens, presidents,
Rulers of states or ordinary folks,
But the worst are hummingbirds of religion,
Especially those who wave a bible in one hand,
But wield deceit in men and women's hearts,
The very scoundrels to whom Rosie,
The Beautiful One, had her soul sold.
For, she, too, was fooled like all village folks.
Much like she had others deceived,
Without regard for their wellbeing.

Hours before her assault,
Without her knowledge and choosing,
She had her heart disburdened
          to one such a fellow,
A man who had visited her.
For it was her darkest hours,
When the saintly village trumpeters,
Without her regard,

Had sounded more alarm bells,
Of her assumed misdeeds,
Claiming she had ushered
One villager's untimely death.
But I, being of sound mind,
I did question this new charge,
A rumour of which Eliab had spoken,
That spelled absolute falsehood!
Hungry ears swallowed this rumour,
Like starved knaves that needed feeding,
Hence, her isolation was fated,
Like no other time in her life.

Almost immediately,
Following this new gossip,
Loneliness wrapped its arms
Around her like a blanket.
With her body ravaged by illness,
She became an easy target,
For an unsavoury man's salvation promise,
By his design, her damnation.

The village Preacher man,
A paragon of deception,
Did his calling make,
Not empty-handed,
But armed with a cell phone,
As proof of his sly mind.
The very hour of his visit,
When crickets hummed the night away,

And darkness had overcome sunlight,
Was as peculiar as his quest.
He stole stealthily to her home,
Clad in his navy-blue pants.
A patch of pink gum,
Stuck to his bums like a cobbler's wax,
Indicated he didn't care about looks.
His misshaped red T-shirt couldn't cover it!
A forest green jacket twice his size
Hang loosely over his thin frame.
And that wasn't all!
The soles of his shoes
Were utterly worn out,

Despite it all,
He walked with the grit
Of a man on a mission.
With his hands in his pocket,
He toyed with his cell phone.
When he arrived at her home,
He gently tapped at her wooden door.
Then, there was silence.
He waited for a fraction of a second.
Hearing no response,
He tapped the door again.
Hodi! Hodi! he said.
There was no sound.
Is anyone home? he said.
Who is there?
Came a shrill voice from inside.

It is me, he said. The village Preacher!
Hung on! the voice said.

Silence followed—
The Preacher patiently stood in wait.
Before long,
The rattling of a lock was all he heard.
Then, Rosie pulled her door open.
A cool draft swept through the house,
As the pious man stepped inside.
She did not need to question him,
For a just reason of his late visit,
But offered him a seat by the door,
Which he took with grace.
Preachers of good repute,
As she knew,
Didn't need a reason to visit their flock.
It was what they did!
Still, this village Preacher wasn't ordinary.

Rosie's living room,
Dimly lit by solar light,
Was less comforting.
For neither she nor he
Dwelt on this detail,
Instead, they mutely sized each other.

When he broke into speech,
The village Preacher said,
Mum, I heard you are unwell!

She, as though lacking in speech,
Nodded her agreement.
I have come to fellowship, he said.
Ahaa! She said. I see!
And pray with you too, he added.
You are so kind, she said,
Wrapping her arms around her body.
No Mum, he said. Thank you,
For allowing me to fellowship with you.
His sweet tongue, as sweet as honey,
Reeled her into his bosom,
And in return, he promised her the world,
Much like she had Eliab—
That he would her soul usher
Its redemption on the chariots of glory.
And in this quest for her saving,
He did the Beautiful One entreat.

Mum, he said.
In the most endearing of voices.
Let us pray!
Yes, son, she said with a whimper.
Prayers are good for the soul.
After our prayer, he said.
Don't shy away from speaking,
Of your troubles, Mum!
        [A soundless Rosie,
            Looked on and without reaction.]
His eyes, two drills,
Made a clean sweep of her fledgling body,

From head-to-toe and settled on her eyes.
His eyes pierced hers.
She, in response,
Dropped her eyes to the floor out of fear,
Of the power his eyes held over her.
That her deepest secrets,
Those to which Adonis never had privy,
Would, in her now, become alive,
No sooner they fell off her lips,
Mainly in her confession to the minister,
A truth the Preacher solemnly hoped,
Would, thusly, occur from his homily.

I am here to pray with you, Mum,
The village Preacher said once more.
Yes, son. Please pray away, she said.
Lord knows I need prayers,
We all need prayer to our Maker!
Immediately, he stood up,
And he fell to his sermonizing for her saving.
Mum, the Preacher man said,
The words of the Lord from Psalms 103 say,

> *The Almighty does not treat us as our sins deserve*
> *Or repay us according to our iniquities.*
> *For as high as the heavens are above the earth,*
> *So great is His love for those who fear Him;*
> *As far as the east is from the west,*

So far has He removed our transgressions
    from us.
As a father has compassion on his children,
So the Lord has compassion on those who
    fear Him.
For He knows how we are formed,
He remembers that we are dust.

Mum from Him,
Your deliverance He shall offer!
For He had his son made
His ultimate sacrifice
For humanity's sake so that
In believing in Him we live.
Repent, Mum Rosie,
All your sins tonight and Nyasaye will
His blessings shower upon you
For the forgiveness of your soul.

    [The village Preacher fell silent,
    But his eyes were fixed on Rosie.
    She sat as still as a tree stump,
    But this was her outward appearance,
    For her inner commotion was a vortex!]

The Preacher man's words,
Which cut through her, made her tremble.
He raised his hands above her head,
And with eyes closed,
He broke into a hymn,
Stomping his feet on the ground
Like a possessed madman,
And then broke into song:

> *Deni langu la dhambi, Yesu amelipa.*
>
> *Kwake msalabani, nilipewa uzima.*

A song that proclaimed,
 Jesus died on the cross for all our sins!
And that in his death,
Humanity was saved from damnation.
Then, the words that flew off his lips
Were strange and unintelligible,
Words only he understood:

> *Sandarara al haj Jehovah babatu!*
>
> *Mtumwa wako! Shandilyamai!*
>
> *Shundai muyanze, arikazi babatu Jehova!*
>
> Nyasaye *does not hide his scars!*
>
> *Sandarara sandiriri!*

He worked himself into a frenzy,
Frothing by the mouth.
And when he stopped,
With all his energy overspent,
He reverted to the bible for Nyasaye's words,
For he knew and believed these words—
Nyasaye's words—were magical.
Making minor changes to the scripture,
He began:

> *Dear heavenly Father,*
>
> *Be merciful to my 'Mum' here,*
>
> *O Nyasaye Baba, Holy Father!*
>
> *Because of your constant love.*
>
> *Because of your great mercy*
>
> *Wipe away her sins for her salvation!*

Wash away all her evil ways
And make her clean from her sins Lord.
Heal her body,
Oh, Dear Jehovah the Almighty!
Sandarara sandiriri al Jehovah babatu, Amen!
He dropped into his chair like a log,
And pushed his back deep into it.
He fished out a hankie from his pocket,
To dry his sweaty brow,
And he returned it.
He let out a deep sigh,
Maybe it was one of relief,
Certain his knife,
A dagger in holiness,
He had into her heart stabbed,
Led her like a cow to the riverside!
Now, she only had to drink from it,
Quench her parched throat,
Sipping on the sweet elixir of salvation.
Mum, the Preacher said.
May I please have some water?
Certainly, she said.

Then,
Rosie rose from her seat,
And silently exited the room.
While in her absence,
He did the unthinkable!
He reached out for his black Nokia,
Unlocked and glanced at it.

Then,
He pressed the record button,
Set it on the table gingerly,
And sat demurely, as though,
He had done nothing,
As he waited for her return,
Having set his bait for her framing.

When she did make her reentry,
With a glass of water in hand,
She handed it to the holy man,
Who gulped it up as fast as he got it,
Every drop of it, like a thirsty donkey.
He placed the glass on the table,
A small old rough piece of furniture!
No one would save for its owner,
Knew its worth,
A father's gift to a daughter,
 A form of his approval of her marriage.

Interestingly,
This very table,
With its rough edges,
Was a sad reminder,
Of the truths about her marriage.
That though it promised stability,
It had more rough edges,
That she couldn't have predicted,
And had caused her more grief than joy!

With the cunningness of a fox,
The Preacher Man said,
Mum, the village has not been kind to you.
Spoken ill of you for years, not in kindness!
I am aware of that, the Beautiful One said.
What can you tell me about this? he said.
What I have to say doesn't matter, she said.
It matters to me, he said.
What difference does it make? she said.
A lot, he said.
I see, she said.

> *[Then, there was a prolonged pause,*
> *As kind of tension followed,*
> *Which one could cut with a knife rose.]*

In good faith, he said.
I am the only one still drawn to your story.
What good does that do for me? she said.
Nothing, but I can help you, he said.
What kind of help can you offer me?
Peace of mind, he said, frothing at the mouth.
Hasn't *the* village already indicated me? she said.
I am not the village, he said. I am a man of Nyasaye's.
You could have fooled me, she said.
I don't care about the village, he said.
Only your soul matters to me!
I'll take my chances with the Devil, she said.
I disagree with you, he said.
Well, I might as well go to Mung'oma,
Cradle home of Mlogooli, our forefather.
Pray to him for my healing and dignity.

I disagree, he said.
No one can give you dignity,
Only you can claim it, he added.
Grab it in both of your arms!
For whatever it is worth,
Please save your soul! he pleaded.
My soul? she said in fury.
My soul is *just* perfectly fine!
I see, he said.
Perfection belongs only to Nyasaye,
Not humankind.
As for your purported dignity, she said,
You can take it and shove it!
I see, the Preacher man said,
Weighing her words in dismay.
I can't change people's views of me, she said.
Their perceptions of me, she said defiantly,
Can't and will never be my reality and measure!
I am on your side Mum,
the Preacher Man said.

    [Rosie, the Beautiful One,

        doubted the preacher's feigned honesty.]

You, too, believe the rumours about me,
Don't you? Be honest, she said.
What I believe doesn't matter, he said.
I am here to listen to you, not condemn!
Really? she said. If it is not a wolf
In sheep's clothing, I don't know! she said.
In the absence of any other truth,
What else is left? he said.

[Rosie didn't respond to the Preacher,
Instead, she withdrew into a deep silence,
And when she opened her lips in speech,
She did so from the depth of her heart!]

The truth, she said.
No one cares about Truth!
Mark my words, the *truth*, my son,
Couldn't be stranger than fiction.
Honestly,
I doubt if you can handle the truth!
Try me, he said.
My wide-opened ears are ready, I swear,
To take it in, and eat every word, he said.

I have done so many things, she said—
The bad, the good, and the ugly—
In my short life here on this earth . . .
Yes, Mum, the Preacher said,
		Eager in anticipation.
Some have been good and others,
My enemies have judged them very badly,
But those phony rascals,
Those who speak ill of me,
I swear are no saints! she said.
If you say so,
Prove them wrong then,
The Preacher man said.
What for? Rosie said.
They are no better than me,
And me than them!

[Hearing this, the Preacher man's ears,
Which were already open, opened wider.
He leaned in closer, stooped a bit forward,
Dropped his eyes onto his phone,
But didn't touch it.]

Yes, she said with **sadness.**

I have done many **bad things!**

What might those be,

The Preacher man **pressed on.**

[A meaningful sly smile formed on his face.
This was a moment for which he had
wished.]

Tell you what, she **said.**

Show me anyone clean in this village,

Free from faults, or **saintly folks.**

[A row of villagers flashed the Preacher's
mind—
Jozam Azere, Jane Mbega, Jeriza Migede,
Joshua Asudi, and many more great men
and women of good repute,
But he couldn't claim they were saintly!]

Tell me, Rosie said,

Any being who hasn't wronged another!

No! I cannot, he said.

Tell me about any soul from this village,

Just *one* who hasn't wronged another?

[The Preacher man did not mutter a word,
But he remained muted by Rosie's train of
thought.
For he had hoped for her easy confession,

*But it wasn't as easy as a wink nor
forthcoming.]*
Is there such a person in this village,
Free from fault? she demanded.
You see, we are all not saints!
      *[Her tone carried with it the weight
      of defiance.]*
I am not talking about the village,
    the Preacher man said.
True, she said.
I know what they say behind my back.
I am no saint and never claimed to be one,
Neither is any other living soul in this village!
I didn't claim you were a saint,
The Preacher protested.
We are all sinners, she said.
I couldn't agree more with you! he said,
But . . .
      [She cut him short.]
Show me a person from this village,
Who is free from any wrongdoing?
Then, she added,
As Nyasaye is my witness,
I'll show you a liar!
I hear you, the Preacher man said,
His tone was one of defeat.
      *[Aware he couldn't get a desired confession,
      He ended his inquiry with Rosie,
      But he hoped to return.]*
Mum Rosie, the Preacher said,

I see you are very tired.

She nodded her agreement.

Since the evening is already spent,

Let me beg my departure,

But I leave you in Nyasaye's hands.

May He bless you abundantly.

May He have mercy on your soul,

      now and forever!

Amen, she said,

But before you depart, *Son*,

Let me tell you a little story,

One my grandmother told me long ago—

> *'Ikizyeezye bird, which dwelt among men,*
>
> *Built herself a nest in the wall of a court of justice.*
>
> *Inside, she laid her eggs and hatched two chicks.*
>
> *Just then, a serpent slithering past the nest,*
>
> *Saw the chicks, glided inside, and ate both.*
>
> *When the bird returned to an empty nest, she cried,*
>
> *Woe to me an alien in this place where all others'*
>
> *Rights are protected, but I alone should suffer!*
>
> *My son, I am that Ikizyeezye wrongfully accused.'*

Son, she said. Go in PEACE!

Peace be with you, too! he said.

Nyasaye *nayaanza* – God willing - I shall return.

> *[He bowed his goodbye,*
> *But Rosie sat still,*
> *As her mind drifted off*
> *Into her heart's darkness,*
> *As dark as the night,*
> *Which swallowed the Preacher in his exit].*

When the Preacher man left
Rosie's house hurriedly,
Nighttime had already fallen,
And the earth was pitch black,
Countless stars dotted Ngoroke village,
Twirled and danced along the skyline.
Any other night,
He might have gone directly to his house.
Not on this night.
Instead,
He marched to his uncle's home,
Bearing his proof,
Of Rosie's *admitted* guilt
Of all her foibles, whatever those were—
For his uncle had earlier challenged him
> when he claimed,
'I alone can make the Beautiful One
 Admit her assumed natural guilt!'
As proof of his prowess—
Of having the ability to change minds,
Make the most obstinate of humankind
To admit the follies of their hearts.
His heart thumped his glee,

As he made his way to his uncle's home.
He couldn't walk there fast enough,
Ready to share his recorded dialogue.
And upon arrival,
He fished his Nokia out of his pocket,
And pressed play,
But the horror-stricken expression
On his face spoke volumes,
For he hadn't recorded a sound.
What a sham for a truth seeker!

11

Innocence Long Lost

That very same night,
After the village Preacher left,
Rosie, the Beautiful One,
Sat still in her room,
Frozen in time and in her seat,
As though fossilized.
She had buried her ailing,
Frail body deep into her chair,
That was stone cold, hard, and rough,
From which she derived no pleasure.

She had no plan, whatsoever,
To turn off her dimly lit lights.
Instead, she closed her eyes,
And frame-by-frame,
Replayed her brief encounter
     with the village Preacher—
Whose hasty probe into her faults—
Seemed as hollow as the soul of an echo!
Of the whispers of her assumed evil deeds,
Behind open and closed doors,
That had not escaped her ears.
For malicious folks had their point made,
That she, the sweet saintly Devil,

Deserved no human touch,
That her flesh they could,
Without her regard, scratch and lacerate,
Or nail her on the cross of shame.
And whom, decisively, named
Was a sassy, airheaded, trampy Jezebel
Labels made against any daughter
Of woman without merit hurt,
As though she were like Morus,
The mighty Greek goddess of doom,
Capable of moving an alp,
And now chastised for every bad thing,
Small or big to ever befall the village.

That,
When a drought came
And destroyed crops and animals,
Folks claimed she had her filthy hand in it!
When a thunderous storm
Tore apart a neighbour's tree,
Bursting it into a million pieces
And peeled its bark,
Like a mother peels a cassava tuber,
The village claimed,
It was her untamable breath to blame,
Intending to do its owner irrevocable harm!
When a roofer fell off a church to his demise,
They said it was the might of her handiwork.

You see,
Charges against her had no limits!
Except, this daughter of woman
Was neither deaf nor blind.
She was not immune to mounting,
Unwarranted pressure wielded against her!
Not even the rumoured attacks
Against her, justified or phony.
She took this unnecessary roughness,
With stride and the gracefulness of a saint.

This night,
As she sat in her dimly lit room,
Her mind hovered between sleep
And wakefulness, as her past,
Her troublesome past flashed,
Gushed out like a flooded river—
Of an image of a dead girl,
Whose sketched silhouette flashed like mist,
And floated on her mind,
As her porcelain brown face,
Teary-eyed, were in repose laid,
And mockingly teased her,
As though the girl's tears were real!
As real as the stars in the galaxy,
But the dead don't cry!
She thought amid sobs.
Her rib-walled heart ached,
As a chill came over her—
Against the warmth—

Of her twin running rivers,
Aware of vindictive minds against her
Are as changeless as the ray of light.
She cringed in her mounting silence,
And her ever-present sorrow!

Then her thoughts,
Of the dead girl faded away,
As fast as a passing breath,
Morphing into the sheer form of a boy,
Whose blurry features were peculiar,
Unusual and indistinguishable
To her troubled mind,
But soon changed
        into her grandson's image,
A grief-shattering specter,
Loaded with a vile charge,
Which in her heart-of-hearts,
Turned her stomach.
While in her mind's eye,
She felt the grotesqueness of the charge.
She, a mother, and grandmother,
Couldn't have stooped too low,
Peculiarly to harm her very own.
What a barbaric and bestial charge!
No pleas of her virtues could
        right this wrong.
The village's cruel defilement charge
Against her of the boy was her heart's dagger,
A lie not even the village Preacher Man,

If he were not a holy Devil himself,
Could not her defence plead,
He, her Judas incarnated,
Poured more acid to an already
      acrid situation!

What a farce!
What a freaking manacle farce!
Then,
She thought of her grandson's simple
      lies to debacle,
Recalling as one is bent to recall such things,
With deep-seated fondness—
Of how she had,
When he was a baby,
Cupped his head in her palms,
Hands so soft and as warm as wool
And like a bird's nest, his security net.
He, as tiny as a squab,
Loved the warmth
And the softness of those hands.
Eye-to-eye,
She oft gazed into his eyes with love,
Albeit hers he, too, cherished,
While she chewed food
And fed him for his nourishment,
Cooed over him like any mother would,
Or like a pigeon cooing over its squabs,
Humming soothing nursery rhymes
And lulling him to sleep,

As any grandmother to grandchild!
    [Ndooro mbombera mwana
    Ndooro mbombera mwana—
    Sleep, lull my child to sleep!]
On this dark night-time,
As she sat in the stillness of her night,
And the rivers of her eyes overflowed,
She thought of how callous the village
Drummers had drummed her verdict!
And crucified her unjustly.

On this dark night-time
She felt the walls of her life
Had caved in tightly against her,
Smothering and suffocating her.
Thus, she solemnly closed this window,
    of her visions,
    of her life's sad saga,
Aware dignity was her saving grace,
Nothing more and forever more,
As she watched her lights flicker
On and off at the dawn of night.
❖

Eliab's image, too, flashed in her mind.
'Aah, the follies of youth,' she thought
His red-hot eyes zeroing in on her,
Fist shaking and chest-thumping,
He demanded his due rights.
No civilities are necessary for this raging bull.
How wrong he had been about her!

How truly wrong he had been,
Vilified the very hand,
Which had his comfort offered frankly,
For had he dared to ask her,
Desired the truth . . . The whole truth,
Nothing more, but the truth.
She could have told him.
The purest of *this* truth he demanded.

Unfortunately,
Truth like the sun cannot perish,
Coveted by all even though elusive.
And to Eliab, how elusive it was!
How could he have known . . .
That while he was incarcerated,
And the jailer's unmerciful hands
Rained blows against his back,
Due price of his robbery,
His parents had his wealth wasted.
Their relentless demand for his money—
From Rosie wasn't without threats
          of bodily harm
Which yielded their desired results.
Thus, she surrendered it *all* to them,
Never spending a penny of it.
Thus, when it mattered, as it ought,
She lacked guts to tell Eliab the truth,
Or to stake her defence.
For she had no fairies to fan luck her way,
In the name of family,

She accepted her assumed guilt,
And saved a home to her damnation,
Preferring to sacrifice her mortality,
Despite her humanistic follies.

Outside,
The night was still,
Mired by a sinister blackness,
But her unwilling mind yielded to her distress,
Yearning to cling onto something . . .
Anything tangible,
To ease the burdens of her heart.

Therefore,
She, like one for whom all was lost,
Closed her ears to the world,
But riled up by her purring mind—
Filled with voices—village voices,
All-knowing voices,
Which *knew* more about her than herself—
And wearisome voices.
She forced her eyelids, heavy with sleep,
To rest against her tired eyes.
She slept only a few hours.
These were troubled hours,
Vision filled, reel-by-reel frames,
Of her past worthy of forgetting
That took centrefold of her now!
It wasn't as visions of her body,
Halo-like, floating above her!

12

Sweet Justice Served Cold

As the dawn hour approached
And Rosie's solar lights went out,
She shifted her weight in her seat,
But her eyes remained closed,
As though she was waiting for someone,
Or something special to possess her.

She pressed her back deep into her seat,
And rested her head on its hard
      warm rough surface.
Whilst, outside,
Heavy mist dripped like rain
Against the peaks of the hills.
Rosie, the Beautiful One,
Who hadn't moved all night long,
Hadn't noticed her lamp's extinguished light.
Neither had she seen the faint slants
      of light flitter inside,
Through the cracks in her windows.
Instead, she pushed her back further,
And further onto its hardened surface
And fell sullenly still as a tomb,
Save for the denseness of the air,

All around and about her,
Nothing to speak of happened.

Outside,
The blackness of night,
Which had cloaked the earth like a blanket,
Had now folded into a copper hue,
As the sun struggled to peek above the hills,
But not bright enough to shower
The skyline with its shimmering glow
Against its massive spread of dark grey.
         [Meanwhile]
At this very dawn hour,
Eliab, like a somnambulist,
Detangled himself from his wrinkled sheets.
His avenging mind was already made up,
And his ears fed up with noble *truths*—
That the villagers' tongues,
         as slippery as ice,
Had his mind tamed and twisted,
And now had himself installed,
As judge, jury, and executor of justice.
Done in the honor of all luckless souls,
Who had fallen prey to an unjust world,
Of Rosie, the capricious evil dame,
Undeserving of life or living,
Whom he thought ought to be stamped out,
Squashed like a bug!

Imali J. Abala

His once brilliant eyes were dulled
With revenge and he, soldier-like,
Frog-marched out of his shanty house.
The cool dawn air whipped at his exposed skin,
But it neither soothed nor pacified his rage.
As he advanced to Rosie's home, his feet in ire,
Stabbed hard at the dew-covered grassy ground,
The element of surprise, his defence.
While the village, still cloaked in slumber,
Would his protection be,
A moment of sheer triumph,
Unaware revenge was a fool's paradise.

In his left hand,
He carried with him a weapon of choice,
        a machete.
The whipping wind made his eyes water,
And his nose ran, but he pressed on,
Aware of the nobility of his action,
That each village deserved its own Achilles,
Whom his legacy will, in their hearts,
        be enshrined.
A man who, with valour, had his village
        saved in blood.
Yet, with all the villagers dead asleep
And no one to bear witness,
Knew the rosy head of Rosie,
Was all he desired for his glory.

The hill's usual dew-covered
      glittery glare reddened
As the sun's shards of red cast
A dazzling glow on the horizon.
Eliab, bull-charged,
Turned into Rosie's compound.
Her house, still shrouded in darkness,
Had the semblance of death.
Never pausing to inspect the surroundings,
Eliab banged on her door.
It wasn't a type of knock that solicited
      an amiable admission,
But police-like; it rattled her door noisily.
He didn't wait for a call of his admittance.
Instead, with his right foot with bulldozer force,
      he smashed it in.
As he busted the door open,
Its wood shattered into a dozen pieces,
And startled the home's sole occupant
From her deep recessed mind,
But she didn't move a muscle.
For she had no time to make peace
      with her Maker!
With the speed of light,
Her assailant's punishing hands
Rained successive blows against her ailing body.
She withdrew into silence,
Clutching in her two hands
Memories of her past
Of truths almost long forgotten

Of her people's strong belief
In the sanctity of life,
Sacred and as precious as gold
Treasured and not destroyed
No matter the cause,
      just or unjust.

Rosie knew as she knew herself,
That to end one's life,
A vile crime among Logooli people,
Was a taboo, a detested offense,
Against the land and the living.
No nobody dared to transgress,
Of which everlasting damnation
Was a lasting wage for offenders.
In taking her life, Rosie knew
That Eliab, as he struck her,
Blow after blow in his revenge
He, wittingly, sentenced himself,
Perhaps, to a worse fate than hers,
For which the villagers and earth
Would mourn in the aftermath,
Even if exacted in follies of youth!

Eliab struck her time and again,
As she let out a mind-shattering scream,
And awakened the slumbering village.
Thus, as her mind tethered
On the void of nothingness,
She softly mumbled,

Aah! Nyasaye knows, as I know myself,
That I am an innocent woman,
And surrendered her ghost.
Eliab's red-covered machete
Hang mid-air at her pronouncement!

148

Epilogue

When Eliab awakened
Nighttime had fallen against the sunless sky.
His body shivered like a swimmer
After a first plunge into a frigid lake
While inwardly,
He wondered if the Devil's radio
Had not poisoned his mind,
Against Rosie, the Beautiful one.
That, maybe, *only* maybe,
This daughter of woman
Had been left for the hanging
At the altar of disgrace and shame!
This thought nagged him
To his very own sad end decades later.

Yet,
As Mama often said,
One can often find a sliver of truth
Amid obscured expressed views.
That truth, like a torch,
Even against Ngoroke mongers,
Never faulters in gleaming
Ultimate Truth amid darkness.
Even though laced with falsehood!

Glossary

Ikizyeezye –	a small black and white bird with a long tail.
Ilikoola –	A dry banana fibre. To "cut *ilikoola*" refers to the first time a woman has intimacy with a man after the burial of her husband.
Imbiring'ong'o –	A type of deadly poison often associated with snake poisoning.
Isugudi –	A traditional Logooli drum.
Kipya kinyemi ingawa kidonda -	A new thing can be a source of joy even if sore.
Matatu –	A van used for public transportation.
Muleembe –	It is a form of greeting meaning peace.
Mileembe –	Peace
Ndendeyi hera ku umuteembe –	Mumps should remain on *umuteembe* tree.
Ndendeyi/ Zindendeyi –	Mumps
Ndooro mbombera mwana –	Sleep, lull my child to sleep.
Nyasaye –	God
Oyoya ovosera ni vusunduki ku kevooya mba –	Do no cry over spilt milk.

Ugali –	A common maize meal in Kenya.
Uvuchima vujila nguza vukusambiila ki –	We should not worry about things that do not concern us.
Waragi –	An alcoholic local brew.

About the Author

Imali J. Abala was born in Western Kenya and currently lives in the United States. She is a professor of English at Ohio Dominican University (USA) where she teaches literature, creative writing, and college writing courses. She is the author of many books; *Haughty Boys of Ngoroke* (Nsemia Inc., 2015), *The Dreamer* (Nsemia Inc., 2017). Collection of children's stories; *Moody Mood and Red Round Ball* , *Moody Mood and Courage, Moody Mood and Jumbo the Bully. Drum Bits of Terror, A Fallen Citadel* (a poetry collection), *Jahenda The Teenage Mother* (Nsemia Inc., 2021), and *The Disinherited and Move on, Trufosa.* Some of her other works have also appeared in Out of the Depth: *Poetry of Poverty, Courage and Resilience, Anthology of Contemporary Short Stories, and Poems from East Africa, A Thousand Voices Rising, and Reflections:* An Anthology by African Women Poets. Imali also co-edited (with Chris Okemwa) *In the Murk of Life* (Nsemia Inc., 2019). and her most recent poetry collection *Unchartered Mind* (Nsemia Inc., 2022). Finally, *The Unforgotten* (Nsemia Inc., 2023).